With love to

_____

_____

DATE

_____

FROM

THE Five LOVE LANGUAGES

How to Express Heartfelt Commitment to Your Mate

GARY CHAPMAN

NORTHFIELD PUBLISHING
CHICAGO

Book Interior Design: *www.designbyjulia.com*

Heart Image © Corbis, Flower Images © Ablestock.com

Jacket Design: *Smartt Guys*

Cover Image © Michael Powers/Index Stock

ISBN: 1-881273-62-8
EAN/ISBN-13: 978-1-881273-62-2

9 10

Printed in the United States of America

To Karolyn,
Shelley, and Derek

CONTENTS

ACKNOWLEDGMENTS

Love begins, or should begin, at home. For me that means Sam and Grace, Dad and Mom, who have loved me for more than fifty years. Without them I would still be seeking love instead of writing about it. Home also means Karolyn, to whom I have been married for more than forty years. If all wives loved as she does, fewer men would be looking over the fence. Shelley and Derek are now out of the nest, exploring new worlds, but I feel secure in the warmth of their love. I am blessed and grateful.

I am indebted to a host of professionals who have influenced my concepts of love. Among them are psychiatrists Ross Campbell, Judson Swihart, and Scott Peck. For editorial assistance, I am indebted to Debbie Barr and Cathy Peterson. The technical expertise of Tricia Kube and Don Schmidt made it possible to meet publication deadlines. Last, and most important, I want to express my gratitude to the hundreds of couples who, over the past thirty years, have shared the intimate side of their lives with me. This book is a tribute to their honesty.

THE FIVE LOVE LANGUAGES

*What Happens to
Love After the Wedding?*

WHAT HAPPENS TO LOVE AFTER THE WEDDING?

At 30,000 feet, somewhere between Buffalo and Dallas, he put his magazine in his seat pocket, turned in my direction, and asked, "What kind of work do you do?"

"I do marriage counseling and lead marriage enrichment seminars," I said matter-of-factly.

"I've been wanting to ask someone this for a long time," he said. "What happens to the love after you get married?"

Relinquishing my hopes of getting a nap, I asked, "What do you mean?"

"Well," he said, "I've been married three times, and each time, it was wonderful before we got married, but somehow after the wedding it all fell apart. All the love I thought I had for her and the love she seemed to have for me evaporated. I am a fairly intelligent person. I operate a successful business, but I don't understand it."

THE SUNFLOWER: "Adoration, Pride, Sunshine."

"How long were you married?" I asked.

"The first one lasted about ten years. The second time, we were married three years, and the last one, almost six years."

"Did your love evaporate immediately after the wedding, or was it a gradual loss?" I inquired.

"Well, the second one went wrong from the very beginning. I don't know what happened. I really thought we loved each other, but the honeymoon was a disaster, and we never recovered. We only dated six months. It was a whirlwind romance. It was really exciting! But after the marriage, it was a battle from the beginning.

"In my first marriage, we had three or four good years before the baby came. After the baby was born, I felt like she gave her attention to the baby and I no longer mattered. It was as if her one goal in life was to have a baby, and after the baby, she no longer needed me."

"Did you tell her that?" I asked.

"Oh, yes, I told her. She said I was crazy. She said I did not under-stand the stress of being a twenty-four-hour nurse. She said I should be more understanding and help her more. I really tried, but it didn't seem to make any difference. After that, we just grew further apart. After a while, there was no love left, just deadness. Both of us agreed that the marriage was over.

"My last marriage? I really thought that one would be different. I had been divorced for three years. We dated each other for two years. I really thought we knew what we were doing, and I thought that perhaps for the first time I really knew what it meant to love someone. I genuinely felt that she loved me.

"After the wedding, I don't think I changed. I continued to express love to her as I had before marriage. I told her how beautiful she was. I told her how much I loved her. I told her how proud I was to be her husband. But a few months after marriage, she started complaining; about petty things at first—like my not taking the garbage out or not hanging up my clothes. Later, she went to attacking my character, telling me she didn't feel she could trust me, accusing me of not being faithful to her. She became a totally negative person. Before marriage, she was never negative. She was one of the most positive people I have ever met. That is one of the things that attracted me to her. She never complained about anything. Everything I did was wonderful, but once we were married, it seemed I could do nothing right. I honestly don't know what happened. Eventually, I lost my love for her and began to resent her. She obviously had no love for me. We agreed there was no benefit to our living together any longer, so we split.

"That was a year ago. So my question is, What happens to love after the wedding? Is my experience common? Is that why we have so many divorces in our country? I can't believe that it happened to me three times. And those who don't divorce, do they learn to live with the emptiness, or does love really stay alive in some marriages? If so, how?"

The questions my friend seated in 5A was asking are the questions that thousands of married and divorced persons are asking today. Some are asking friends, some are asking counselors and clergy, and some are asking themselves. Sometimes the answers are couched in psychological research jargon that is almost incomprehensible. Sometimes they are couched in humor and folklore. Most of the jokes and pithy sayings contain some truth, but they are like offering an aspirin to a person with cancer.

The desire for romantic love in marriage is deeply rooted in our psychological makeup. Almost every popular magazine has at least one article each issue on keeping love alive in a marriage. Books abound on the subject. Television and radio talk shows deal with it. Keeping love alive in our marriages is serious business.

With all the books, magazines, and practical help available, why is it that so few couples seem to have found the secret to keeping love alive after the wedding? Why is it that a couple can attend a communication workshop, hear wonderful ideas on how to enhance communication, return home, and find themselves totally unable to implement the communication patterns demonstrated? How is it that we read a magazine article on "101 Ways to Express Love to Your Spouse," select two or three ways that seem especially good to us, try them, and our spouse doesn't even acknowledge our effort? We give up on the other 98 ways and go back to life as usual.

We must be willing to learn our spouse's primary love language if we are to be effective communicators of love.

The answer to those questions is the purpose of this book. It is not that the books and articles already published are not helpful. The problem is that we have overlooked one fundamental truth: People speak different love languages.

In the area of linguistics, there are major language groups: Japanese, Chinese, Spanish, English, Portuguese, Greek, German,

French, and so on. Most of us grow up learning the language of our parents and siblings, which becomes our primary or native tongue. Later, we may learn additional languages but usually with much more effort. These become our secondary languages. We speak and understand best our native language. We feel most comfortable speaking that language. The more we use a secondary language, the more comfortable we become conversing in it. If we speak only our primary language and encounter someone else who speaks only his or her primary language, which is different from ours, our communication will be limited. We must rely on pointing, grunting, drawing pictures, or acting out our ideas. We can communicate, but it is awkward. Language differences are part and parcel of human culture. If we are to communicate effectively across cultural lines, we must learn the language of those with whom we wish to communicate.

In the area of love, it is similar. Your emotional love language and the language of your spouse may be as different as Chinese from English. No matter how hard you try to express love in English, if your spouse understands only Chinese, you will never understand how to love each other. My friend on the plane was speaking the language of "Affirming Words" to his third wife when he said, "I told her how beautiful she was. I told her I loved her. I told her how proud I was to be her husband." He was speaking love, and he was sincere, but she did not understand his language. Perhaps she was looking for love in his behavior and didn't see it. Being sincere is not enough. We must be willing to learn our spouse's primary love language if we are to be effective communicators of love.

My conclusion after thirty years of marriage counseling is that there are basically five emotional love languages—five ways that people speak and understand emotional love. In the field of linguistics a language may have numerous dialects or variations. Similarly, within the five basic emotional love languages, there are many dialects. That accounts for the magazine articles titled "10 Ways to Let Your Spouse Know You Love Her," "20 Ways to Keep Your Man at Home," or "365

Expressions of Marital Love." There are not 10, 20, or 365 basic love languages. In my opinion, there are only five. However, there may be numerous dialects. The number of ways to express love within a love language is limited only by one's imagination. The important thing is to speak the love language of your spouse.

We have long known that in early childhood development each child develops unique emotional patterns. Some children, for example, develop a pattern of low self-esteem whereas others have healthy self-esteem. Some develop emotional patterns of insecurity whereas others grow up feeling secure. Some children grow up feeling loved, wanted, and appreciated, yet others grow up feeling unloved, unwanted, and unappreciated.

The children who feel loved by their parents and peers will develop a primary emotional love language based on their unique psychological makeup and the way their parents and other significant persons expressed love to them. They will speak and understand one primary love language. They may later learn a secondary love language, but they will always feel most comfortable with their primary language. Children who do not feel loved by their parents and peers will also develop a primary love language. However, it will be somewhat distorted in much the same way as some children may learn poor grammar and have an underdeveloped vocabulary. That poor programming does not mean they cannot become good communicators. But it does mean they will have to work at it more diligently than those who had a more positive model. Likewise, children who grow up with an underdeveloped sense of emotional love can also come to feel loved and to communicate love, but they will have to work at it more diligently than those who grew up in a healthy, loving atmosphere.

Seldom do a husband and wife have the same primary emotional love language. We tend to speak our primary love language, and we become confused when our spouse does not understand what we are communicating. We are expressing our love, but the message does not come through because we are speaking what, to them, is a foreign language. Therein lies the fundamental problem, and it is the purpose of this book to offer a solution. That is why I dare to write another book on love. Once we discover the five basic love languages and understand our own primary love language, as well as the primary love language of our spouse, we will then have the needed information to apply the ideas in the books and articles.

Once you identify and learn to speak your spouse's primary love language, I believe that you will have discovered the key to a long-lasting, loving marriage. Love need not evaporate after the wedding, but in order to keep it alive most of us will have to put forth the effort to learn a secondary love language. We cannot rely on our native tongue if our spouse does not understand it. If we want him/her to feel the love we are trying to communicate, we must express it in his or her primary love language.

THE FIVE LOVE LANGUAGES

Keeping the Love Tank Full

KEEPING THE LOVE TANK FULL

Love is the most important word in the English language —and the most confusing. Both secular and religious thinkers agree that love plays a central role in life. We are told that "love is a many-splendored thing" and that "love makes the world go round." Thousands of books, songs, magazines, and movies are peppered with the word. Numerous philosophical and theological systems have made a prominent place for love. And the founder of the Christian faith wanted love to be the distinguishing characteristic of His followers.[1]

Psychologists have concluded that the need to feel loved is a primary human emotional need. For love, we will climb mountains, cross seas, traverse desert sands, and endure untold hardships. Without love, mountains become unclimbable, seas uncrossable, deserts unbearable, and hardships our plight in life. The Christian apostle to the Gentiles, Paul, exalted love when he indicated that all human accomplishments that are not motivated by love are, in the end, empty. He concluded that in the last scene of the human drama, only three characters will remain: "faith, hope and love. But the greatest of these is love."[2]

WHITE VIOLETS: "Let's take a chance on happiness."

If we can agree that the word *love* permeates human society, both historically and in the present, we must also agree that it is a most confusing word. We use it in a thousand ways. We say, "I love hot dogs," and in the next breath, "I love my mother." We speak of loving activities: swimming, skiing, hunting. We love objects: food, cars, houses. We love animals: dogs, cats, even pet snails. We love nature: trees, grass, flowers, and weather. We love people: mother, father, son, daughter, parents, wives, husbands, friends. We even fall in love with love.

If all that is not confusing enough, we also use the word *love* to explain behavior. "I did it because I love her." That explanation is given for all kinds of actions. A man is involved in an adulterous relationship, and he calls it love. The preacher, on the other hand, calls it sin. The wife of an alcoholic picks up the pieces after her husband's latest episode. She calls it love, but the psychologist calls it codependency. The parent indulges all the child's wishes, calling it love. The family therapist would call it irresponsible parenting. What is loving behavior?

The purpose of this book is not to eliminate all confusion surrounding the word *love*, but to focus on that kind of love that is essential to our emotional health. Child psychologists affirm that every child has certain basic emotional needs that must be met if he is to be emotionally stable. Among those emotional needs, none is more basic than the need for love and affection, the need to sense that he or she belongs and is wanted. With an adequate supply of affection, the child will likely develop into a responsible adult. Without that love, he or she will be emotionally and socially retarded.

I liked the metaphor the first time I heard it: "Inside every child is an 'emotional tank' waiting to be filled with love. When a child really feels loved, he will develop normally but when the love tank is empty, the child will misbehave. Much of the misbehavior of children is motivated by the cravings of an empty 'love tank.'" I was listening to Dr. Ross Campbell, a psychiatrist who specializes in the treatment of children and adolescents.

As I listened, I thought of the hundreds of parents who had paraded the misdeeds of their children through my office. I had never visualized an empty love tank inside those children, but I had certainly seen the results of it. Their misbehavior was a misguided search for the love they did not feel. They were seeking love in all the wrong places and in all the wrong ways.

I remember Ashley, who at thirteen years of age was being treated for a sexually transmitted disease. Her parents were crushed. They were angry with Ashley. They were upset with the school, which they blamed for teaching her about sex. "Why would she do this?" they asked.

In my conversation with Ashley, she told me of her parents' divorce when she was six years old. "I thought my father left because he didn't love me," she said. "When my mother remarried when I was ten, I felt she now had someone to love her, but I still had no one to love me. I wanted so much to be loved. I met this boy at school. He was older than me, but he liked me. I couldn't believe it. He was kind to me, and in a while I really felt he loved me. I didn't want to have sex, but I wanted to be loved."

Ashley's "love tank" had been empty for many years. Her mother and stepfather had provided for her physical needs but had not realized the deep emotional struggle raging inside her. They certainly loved Ashley, and they thought that she felt their love. Not until it was almost too late did they discover that they were not speaking Ashley's primary love language.

The emotional need for love, however, is not simply a childhood phenomenon. That need follows us into adulthood and into marriage. The "in love" experience temporarily meets that need, but it is inevitably a "quick fix" and, as we shall learn later, has a limited and predictable life span. After we come down from the high of the "in love" obsession, the emotional need for love resurfaces because it is fundamental to our nature. It is at the center of our emotional desires. We needed love before we "fell in love," and we will need it as long as we live.

At the heart of mankind's existence is the desire to be intimate and to be loved by another. Marriage is designed to meet that need for intimacy and love.

The need to feel loved by one's spouse is at the heart of marital desires. A man said to me recently, "What good is the house, the cars, the place at the beach, or any of the rest of it if your wife doesn't love you?" Do you understand what he was really saying? "More than anything, I want to be loved by my wife." Material things are no replacement for human, emotional love. A wife says, "He ignores me all day long and then wants to jump in bed with me. I hate it." She is not a wife who hates sex; she is a wife desperately pleading for emotional love.

Something in our nature cries out to be loved by another. Isolation is devastating to the human psyche. That is why solitary confinement is considered the cruelest of punishments. At the heart of mankind's existence is the desire to be intimate and to be loved by another. Marriage is designed to meet that need for intimacy and love. That is why the ancient biblical writings spoke of the husband and wife becoming "one flesh." That did not mean that individuals would lose their identity; it meant that they would enter into each other's lives in a deep and intimate way. The New Testament writers challenged both the husband and the wife to love each other. From Plato to Peck, writers have emphasized the importance of love in marriage.

But, if love is important, it is also elusive. I have listened to many married couples share their secret pain. Some came to me because the inner ache had become unbearable. Others came because they realized that their behavior patterns or the misbehavior of their spouse was destroying the marriage. Some came simply to inform me that they no longer wanted to be married. Their dreams of "living happily ever after" had been dashed against the hard walls of reality. Again and again I have heard the words "Our love is gone, our relationship is dead. We used to feel close, but not now. We no longer enjoy being with each other. We don't meet each other's needs." Their stories bear testimony that adults as well as children have "love tanks."

Could it be that deep inside hurting couples exists an invisible "emotional love tank" with its gauge on empty? Could the misbehavior, withdrawal, harsh words, and critical spirit occur because of that empty tank? If we could find a way to fill it, could the marriage be reborn? With a full tank would couples be able to create an emotional climate where it is possible to discuss differences and resolve conflicts? Could that tank be the key that makes marriage work?

Those questions sent me on a long journey. Along the way, I discovered the simple yet powerful insights contained in this book. The journey has taken me not only through thirty years of marriage counseling but into the hearts and minds of hundreds of couples throughout America. From Seattle to Miami, couples have invited me into the inner chamber of their marriages, and we have talked openly. The illustrations included in this book are cut from the fabric of real life. Only names and places are changed to protect the privacy of the individuals who have spoken so freely.

I am convinced that keeping the emotional love tank full is as important to a marriage as maintaining the proper oil level is to an automobile. Running your marriage on an empty "love tank" may cost you even more than trying to drive your car without oil. What you are about to read has the potential of saving thousands of marriages and can even enhance the emotional climate of a good marriage. Whatever the quality of your marriage now, it can always be better.

WARNING: Understanding the five love languages and learning to speak the primary love language of your spouse may radically affect his or her behavior. People behave differently when their emotional love tanks are full.

Before we examine the five love languages, however, we must address one other important but confusing phenomenon: the euphoric experience of "falling in love."

NOTES
1. John 13:35.
2. 1 Corinthians 13:13.

THE FIVE LOVE LANGUAGES

Falling in Love

She showed up at my office without an appointment and asked my secretary if she could see me for five minutes. I had known Janice for eighteen years. She was thirty-six and had never married. She had dated several men through the years, one for six years, another for three years, and several others for shorter periods of time. From time to time, she had made appointments with me to discuss a particular difficulty in one of her relationships. She was by nature a disciplined, conscientious, organized, thoughtful, and caring person. It was completely out of character for her to show up at my office unannounced. I thought, *There must be some terrible crisis for Janice to show up without an appointment.* I told my secretary to show her in, and I fully expected to see her burst into tears and tell me some tragic story as soon as the door was closed. Instead, she virtually skipped into my office, beaming with excitement.

HYACINTH: *"Playful joy."*

"How are you today, Janice?" I asked.

"Great!" she said. "I've never been better in my life. I'm getting married!"

"You are?" I said, revealing my shock. "To whom and when?"

"To David Gallespie," she exclaimed, "in September."

"That's exciting. How long have you been dating?"

"Three weeks. I know it's crazy, Dr. Chapman, after all the people I have dated and the number of times I came so close to getting married. I can't believe it myself, but I know David is the one for me. From the first date, we both knew it. Of course, we didn't talk about it on the first night, but one week later, he asked me to marry him. I knew he was going to ask me, and I knew I was going to say yes. I have never felt this way before, Dr. Chapman. You know about the relationships that I have had through the years and the struggles I have had. In every relationship, something was not right. I never felt at peace about marrying any of them, but I know that David is the right one."

By this time, Janice was rocking back and forth in her chair, giggling and saying, "I know it's crazy, but I am so happy. I have never been this happy in my life."

What has happened to Janice? She has fallen in love. In her mind, David is the most wonderful man she has ever met. He is perfect in every way. He will make the ideal husband. She thinks about him day and night. The facts that David has been married twice before, has three children, and has had three jobs in the past year are trivial to Janice. She's happy, and she is convinced that she is going to be happy forever with David. She is in love.

Most of us enter marriage by way of the "in love" experience. We meet someone whose physical characteristics and personality traits create enough electrical shock to trigger our "love alert" system. The bells go off, and we set in motion the process of getting to know the person. The first step may be sharing a hamburger or steak, depending on our budget, but our real interest is not in the food. We are on a quest to discover *love*. "Could this warm, tingly feeling I have inside be the 'real' thing?"

Sometimes we lose the tingles on the first date. We find out that she dips snuff, and the tingles run right out our toes; we want no more hamburgers with her. Other times, however, the tingles are stronger after the hamburger than before. We arrange for a few more "together" experiences, and before long the level of intensity has increased to the point where we find ourselves saying, "I think I'm falling in love." Eventually we are convinced that it is the "real thing," and we tell the other person, hoping the feeling is reciprocal. If it isn't, things cool off a bit or we redouble our efforts to impress, and eventually win the love of, our beloved. When it is reciprocal, we start talking about marriage because everyone agrees that being "in love" is the necessary foundation for a good marriage.

At its peak, the "in love" experience is euphoric. We are emotionally obsessed with each other. We go to sleep thinking of one another. When we rise that person is the first thought on our minds. We long to be together. Spending time together is like playing in the anteroom of heaven. When we hold hands, it seems as if our blood flows together. We could kiss forever if we didn't have to go to school or work. Embracing stimulates dreams of marriage and ecstasy.

The person who is "in love" has the illusion that his beloved is perfect. His mother can see the flaws but he can't. His mother says, "Darling, have you considered she has been under psychiatric care for five years?" But he replies, "Oh, Mother, give me a break. She's been out for three months now." His friends also can see the flaws but are not likely to tell him unless he asks, and chances are he won't because in his mind she is perfect and what others think doesn't matter.

Our dreams before marriage are of marital bliss: "We are going to make each other supremely happy. Other couples may argue and fight, but not us. We love each other." Of course, we are not totally naive. We know intellectually that we will eventually have differences. But we are certain that we will discuss those differences openly; one of us will always be willing to make concessions, and we will reach agreement. It's hard to believe anything else when you are in love.

Our dreams before marriage are of marital bliss. . . . It's hard to believe anything else when you are in love.

We have been led to believe that if we are really in love, it will last forever. We will always have the wonderful feelings that we have at this moment. Nothing could ever come between us. Nothing will ever overcome our love for each other. We are enamored and caught up in the beauty and charm of the other's personality. Our love is the most wonderful thing we have ever experienced. We observe that some married couples seem to have lost that feeling, but it will never happen to us. "Maybe they did not have the real thing," we reason.

Unfortunately, the eternality of the "in love" experience is fiction, not fact. Dr. Dorothy Tennov, a psychologist, has done long-range studies on the in-love phenomenon. After studying scores of couples, she concluded that the average life span of a romantic obsession is two years. If it is a secretive love affair, it may last a little longer. Eventually, however, we all descend from the clouds and plant our feet on earth again. Our eyes are opened, and we see the warts of the other person. We recognize that some of his/her personality traits are actually irritating. Her behavior patterns are annoying. He has the capacity for hurt and anger, perhaps even harsh words and critical judgments. Those little traits that we overlooked when we were in love now become huge mountains. We remember Mother's words and ask ourselves, *How could I have been so foolish?*

Welcome to the real world of marriage, where hairs are always on the sink and little white spots cover the mirror, where arguments center on which way the toilet paper comes off and whether the lid should be up or down. It is a world where shoes do not walk to the closet and drawers do not close themselves, where coats do not like hangers and socks go AWOL during laundry. In this world, a look can hurt and a word can crush. Intimate lovers can become enemies, and marriage a battlefield.

What happened to the "in love" experience? Alas, it was but an illusion by which we were tricked into signing our names on the dotted line, for better or for worse. No wonder so many have come to curse marriage and the partner whom they once loved. After all, if we were deceived, we have a right to be angry. Did we really have the "real" thing? I think so. The problem was faulty information.

The bad information was the idea that the "in love" obsession would last forever. We should have known better. A casual observation should have taught us that if people remained obsessed, we would all be in serious trouble. The shock waves would rumble through business, industry, church, education, and the rest of society. Why?

Because people who are "in love" lose interest in other pursuits. That is why we call it "obsession." The college student who falls head over heels in love sees his grades tumbling. It is difficult to study when you are in love. Tomorrow you have a test on the War of 1812, but who cares about the War of 1812? When you're in love, everything else seems irrelevant. A man said to me, "Dr. Chapman, my job is disintegrating."

"What do you mean?" I asked.

"I met this girl, fell in love, and I can't get a thing done. I can't keep my mind on my job. I spend my day dreaming about her."

The euphoria of the "in love" state gives us the illusion that we have an intimate relationship. We feel that we belong to each other. We believe we can conquer all problems. We feel altruistic toward each other. As one young man said about his fiancée, "I can't conceive of doing anything to hurt her. My only desire is to make her happy. I would do anything to make her happy." Such obsession gives us the false sense that our egocentric attitudes have been eradicated and we have become sort of a Mother Teresa, willing to give anything for the benefit of our lover. The reason we can do that so freely is that we sincerely believe that our lover feels the same way toward us. We believe that she is committed to meeting our needs, that he loves us as much as we love him and would never do anything to hurt us.

That thinking is always fanciful. Not that we are insincere in what we think and feel, but we are unrealistic. We fail to reckon with the reality of human nature. By nature, we are egocentric. Our world revolves around us. None of us is totally altruistic. The euphoria of the "in love" experience only gives us that illusion.

Once the experience of falling in love has run its natural course (remember, the average in-love experience lasts two years), we will return to the world of reality and begin to assert ourselves. He will express his desires, but his desires will be different from hers. He desires sex, but she is too tired. He wants to buy a new car, but she says, "That's absurd!" She wants to visit her parents, but he says, "I don't like spending so much time with your family." He wants to play in the softball tournament, and she says, "You love softball more than you love me." Little by little, the illusion of intimacy evaporates, and the individual desires, emotions, thoughts, and behavior patterns exert themselves. They are two individuals. Their minds have not melded together, and their emotions mingled only briefly in the ocean of love. Now the waves of reality begin to separate them. They fall out of love, and at that point either they withdraw, separate, divorce, and set off in search of a new in-love experience, or they begin the hard work of learning to love each other without the euphoria of the in-love obsession.

Some researchers, among them psychiatrist M. Scott Peck and psychologist Dorothy Tennov, have concluded that the in-love experience should not be called "love" at all. Dr. Tennov coined the word *limerance* for the in-love experience in order to distinguish that experience from what she considers real love. Dr. Peck concludes that the falling-in-love experience is not real love for three reasons. First, falling in love is not an act of the will or a conscious choice. No matter how much we may want to fall in love, we cannot make it happen. On the other hand, we may not be seeking the experience when it overtakes us. Often, we fall in love at inopportune times and with unlikely people.

Second, falling in love is not real love because it is effortless. Whatever we do in the in-love state requires little discipline or conscious effort on our part. The long, expensive phone calls we make to each other, the money we spend traveling to see each other, the gifts we give, the work projects we do are as nothing to us. As the instinctual nature of the bird dictates the building of a nest, so the instinctual nature of the in-love experience pushes us to do outlandish and unnatural things for each other.

Third, one who is "in love" is not genuinely interested in fostering the personal growth of the other person. "If we have any purpose in mind when we fall in love it is to terminate our own loneliness and perhaps ensure this result through marriage."[1] The in-love experience does not focus on our own growth nor on the growth and development of the other person. Rather, it gives us the sense that we have arrived and that we do not need further growth. We are at the apex of life's happiness, and our only desire is to stay there. Certainly our beloved does not need to grow because she is perfect. We simply hope she will remain perfect.

If falling in love is not real love, what is it? Dr. Peck concludes that it "is a genetically determined instinctual component of mating behavior. In other words, the temporary collapse of ego boundaries that constitutes falling in love is a stereotypic response of human beings to a configuration of internal sexual drives and external sexual stimuli, which serves to increase the probability of sexual pairing and bonding so as to enhance the survival of the species."[2]

Whether or not we agree with that conclusion, those of us who have fallen in love and out of love will likely agree that the experience does catapult us into emotional orbit unlike anything else we have experienced. It tends to disengage our reasoning abilities, and we often find ourselves doing and saying things that we would never have done in more sober moments. In fact, when we come down from the emotional obsession we often wonder why we did those things. When the wave of emotions subsides and we come back to the real world where our differences are illuminated, how many of us have asked, "Why did we get married? We don't agree on anything." Yet, at the height of the in-loveness, we thought we agreed on everything—at least everything that was important.

The in-love experience does not focus on our own growth nor on the growth and development of the other person. Rather, it gives us the sense that we have arrived.

Does that mean that having been tricked into marriage by the illusion of being in love, we are now faced with two options: (1) we are destined to a life of misery with our spouse, or (2) we must jump ship and try again? Our generation has opted for the latter, whereas an earlier generation often chose the former. Before we automatically conclude that we have made the better choice, perhaps we should examine the data. Presently 40 percent of first marriages in this country end in divorce. Sixty percent of second marriages and 75 percent of third marriages end the same way. Apparently the prospect of a happier marriage the second and third time around is not substantial.

Research seems to indicate that there is a third and better alternative: We can recognize the in-love experience for what it was—a temporary emotional high—and now pursue "real love" with our spouse. That kind of love is emotional in nature but not obsessional. It is a love that unites reason and emotion. It involves an act of the will and requires discipline, and it recognizes the need for personal growth. Our most basic emotional need is not to fall in love but to be genuinely loved by another, to know a love that grows out of reason and choice, not instinct. I need to be loved by someone who chooses to love me, who sees in me something worth loving.

That kind of love requires effort and discipline. It is the choice to expend energy in an effort to benefit the other person, knowing that if his or her life is enriched by your effort, you too will find a sense of satisfaction—the satisfaction of having genuinely loved another. It does not require the euphoria of the "in love" experience. In fact, true love cannot begin until the "in love" experience has run its course.

We cannot take credit for the kind and generous things we do while under the influence of "the obsession." We are pushed and carried along by an instinctual force that goes beyond our normal behavior patterns. But if, once we return to the real world of human choice, we choose to be kind and generous, that is real love.

The emotional need for love must be met if we are to have emotional health. Married adults long to feel affection and love from their spouses. We feel secure when we are assured that our mate accepts us, wants us, and is committed to our well-being. During the in-love stage, we felt all of those emotions. It was heavenly while it lasted. Our mistake was in thinking it would last forever.

But that obsession was not meant to last forever. In the textbook of marriage, it is but the introduction. The heart of the book is rational, volitional love. That is the kind of love to which the sages have always called us. It is intentional.

That is good news to the married couple who have lost all of their "in love" feelings. If love is a choice, then they have the capacity to love after the "in love" obsession has died and they have returned to the real world. That kind of love begins with an attitude—a way of thinking. Love is the attitude that says, "I am married to you, and I choose to look out for your interests." Then the one who chooses to love will find appropriate ways to express that decision.

"But it seems so sterile," some may contend. "Love as an attitude with appropriate behavior? Where are the shooting stars, the balloons, the deep emotions? What about the spirit of anticipation, the twinkle of the eye, the electricity of a kiss, the excitement of sex? What about the emotional security of knowing that I am number one in his/her mind?" That is what this book is all about. How do we meet each other's deep, emotional need to feel loved? If we can learn that and choose to do it, then the love we share will be exciting beyond anything we ever felt when we were infatuated.

For many years now, I have discussed the five emotional love languages in my marriage seminars and in private counseling sessions. Thousands of couples will attest to the validity of what you are about to read. My files are filled with letters from people whom I have never

Rational, volitional love . . . is the kind of love to which the sages have always called us.

met, saying, "A friend loaned me one of your tapes on love languages, and it has revolutionized our marriage. We had struggled for years trying to love each other, but our efforts had missed each other emotionally. Now that we are speaking the appropriate love languages, the emotional climate of our marriage has radically improved."

When your spouse's emotional love tank is full and he feels secure in your love, the whole world looks bright and your spouse will move out to reach his highest potential in life. But when the love tank is empty and he feels used but not loved, the whole world looks dark and he will likely never reach his potential for good in the world. In the next five chapters, I will explain the five emotional love languages and then, in chapter 9, illustrate how discovering your spouse's primary love language can make your efforts at love most productive.

NOTES
1. M. Scott Peck, *The Road Less Traveled* (New York: Simon & Schuster, 1978), pp. 89–90.
2. Ibid., p. 90.

THE FIVE LOVE LANGUAGES

WORDS OF AFFIRMATION

Quality Time

Receiving Gifts

Acts of Service

Physical Touch

LOVE LANGUAGE #1: *Words of Affirmation*

Mark Twain once said, "I can live for two months on a good compliment." If we take Twain literally, six compliments a year would have kept his emotional love tank at the operational level. Your spouse will probably need more.

One way to express love emotionally is to use words that build up. Solomon, author of the ancient Hebrew wisdom literature, wrote, "The tongue has the power of life and death."[1] Many couples have never learned the tremendous power of verbally affirming each other. Solomon further noted, "An anxious heart weighs a man down, but a kind word cheers him up."[2]

Verbal compliments, or words of appreciation, are powerful communicators of love. They are best expressed in simple, straightforward statements of affirmation, such as:

THE PANSY: "Thoughtful reflection."

"You look sharp in that suit."

"Do you ever look nice in that dress! Wow!"

"You must be the best potato cook in the world. I love these potatoes."

"I really appreciate your washing the dishes tonight."

"Thanks for getting the baby-sitter lined up tonight. I want you to know I don't take that for granted."

"I really appreciate your taking the garbage out."

What would happen to the emotional climate of a marriage if the husband and wife heard such words of affirmation regularly?

Several years ago, I was sitting in my office with my door open. A lady walking down the hall said, "Have you got a minute?"

"Sure, come in."

She sat down and said, "Dr. Chapman, I've got a problem. I can't get my husband to paint our bedroom. I have been after him for nine months. I have tried everything I know, and I can't get him to paint it."

My first thought was, *Lady, you are at the wrong place. I am not a paint contractor.* But I said, "Tell me about it."

She said, "Well, last Saturday was a good example. You remember how pretty it was? Do you know what my husband did all day long? He washed and waxed the car."

"So what did you do?"

"I went out there and said, 'Bob, I don't understand you. Today would have been a perfect day to paint the bedroom, and here you are washing and waxing the car.'"

"So did he paint the bedroom?" I inquired.

"No. It's still not painted. I don't know what to do."

"Let me ask you a question," I said. "Are you opposed to clean, waxed cars?"

"No, but I want the bedroom painted."

"Are you certain that your husband knows that you want the bedroom painted?"

"I know he does," she said. "I have been after him for nine months."

"Let me ask you one more question. Does your husband ever do anything good?"

"Like what?"

"Oh, like taking the garbage out, or getting bugs off the windshield of the car you drive, or putting gas in the car, or paying the electric bill, or hanging up his coat?"

"Yes," she said, "he does some of those things."

"Then I have two suggestions. One, don't ever mention painting the bedroom again." I repeated, "Don't ever mention it again."

"I don't see how that's going to help," she said.

"Look, you just told me that he knows that you want the bedroom painted. You don't have to tell him anymore. He already knows. The second suggestion I have is that the next time your husband does anything good, give him a verbal compliment. If he takes the garbage out, say, 'Bob, I want you to know that I really appreciate your taking the garbage out.' Don't say, 'About time you took the garbage out. The flies were going to carry it out for you.' If you see him paying the electric bill, put your hand on his shoulder and say, 'Bob, I really appreciate your paying the electric bill. I hear there are husbands who don't do that, and I want you to know how much I appreciate it.' Every time he does anything good, give him a verbal compliment."

"I don't see how that's going to get the bedroom painted."

I said, "You asked for my advice. You have it. It's free."

She wasn't very happy with me when she left. Three weeks later, however, she came back to my office and said, "It worked!" She had learned that verbal compliments are far greater motivators than nagging words.

I am not suggesting verbal flattery in order to get your spouse to do something you want. The object of love is not getting something you want but doing something for the well-being of the one you love. It is a fact, however, that when we receive affirming words we are far more likely to be motivated to reciprocate and do something our spouse desires.

The object of love is not getting something you want but doing something for the well-being of the one you love. It is a fact, however, that when we receive affirming words we are far more likely to be motivated to reciprocate.

Encouraging Words

Giving verbal compliments is only one way to express words of affirmation to your spouse. Another dialect is encouraging words. The word *encourage* means "to inspire courage." All of us have areas in which we feel insecure. We lack courage, and that lack of courage often hinders us from accomplishing the positive things that we would like to do. The latent potential within your spouse in his or her areas of insecurity may await your encouraging words.

Allison had always liked to write. Late in her college career, she took a few courses in journalism. She quickly realized that her excitement about writing exceeded her interest in history, which had been her academic major. It was too late to change majors, but after college and especially before the first baby, she wrote several articles. She submitted one article to a magazine, but when she received a rejection slip, she never had the courage to submit another. Now that the children were older and she had more time to contemplate, Allison was again writing.

Keith, Allison's husband, had paid little attention to Allison's writing in the early days of their marriage. He was busy with his own vocation and caught up in the pressure of climbing the corporate ladder. In time, however, Keith had realized that life's deepest meaning is not found in accomplishments but in relationships. He had learned to give more attention to Allison and her interests. So it was quite natural one night for him to pick up one of Allison's articles and read it. When he finished, he went into the den where Allison was reading a book. With great enthusiasm, he said, "I hate to interrupt your reading, but I have to tell you this. I just finished reading your article on 'Making the Most of the Holidays.' Allison, you are an excellent writer. This stuff ought to be published! You write clearly. Your words paint pictures that I can visualize. You have a fascinating style. You have to submit this stuff to some magazines."

"Do you really think so?" Allison asked hesitantly.

"I know so," Keith said. "I'm telling you, this is good."

When Keith left the room, Allison did not resume her reading. With the closed book in her lap, she dreamed for thirty minutes about what Keith had said. She wondered if others would view her writing the same way he did. She remembered the rejection slip she had received years ago, but she reasoned that she was a different person now. Her writing was better. She had had more experiences. Before she left the chair to get a drink of water, Allison had made a decision. She would submit her articles to some magazines. She would see if they could be published.

Keith's encouraging words were spoken fourteen years ago. Allison has had numerous articles published since then and now has a book contract. She is an excellent writer, but it took the encouraging words from her husband to inspire her to take the first step in the arduous process of getting an article published.

Perhaps your spouse has untapped potential in one or more areas of life. That potential may be awaiting your encouraging words. Perhaps she needs to enroll in a course to develop that potential. Maybe he needs to meet some people who have succeeded in that area, who can give him insight on the next step he needs to take. Your words may give your spouse the courage necessary to take that first step.

Please note that I am not talking about pressuring your spouse to do something that you want. I am talking about encouraging him to develop an interest that he already has. For example, some husbands pressure their wives to lose weight. The husband says, "I am encouraging her," but to the wife it sounds like condemnation. Only when a person wants to lose weight can you give her encouragement. Until she has the desire, your words will fall into the category of preaching. Such words seldom encourage. They are almost always heard as words of judgment, designed to stimulate guilt. They express not love but rejection.

Encouragement requires empathy and seeing the world from your spouse's perspective. We must first learn what is important to our spouse.

If, however, your spouse says, "I think I would like to enroll in a weight-loss program this fall," then you have opportunity to give words of encouragement. Encouraging words would sound like this. "If you decide to do that, I can tell you one thing. You will be a success. That's one of the things I like about you. When you set your mind to something, you do it. If that's what you want to do, I will certainly do everything I can to help you. And don't worry about the cost of the program. If it's what you want to do, we'll find the money." Such words may give your spouse the courage to phone the weight-loss center.

Encouragement requires empathy and seeing the world from your spouse's perspective. We must first learn what is important to our spouse. Only then can we give encouragement. With verbal encouragement, we are trying to communicate, "I know. I care. I am with you. How can I help?" We are trying to show that we believe in him and in his abilities. We are giving credit and praise.

Most of us have more potential than we will ever develop. What holds us back is often courage. A loving spouse can supply that all-important catalyst. Of course, encouraging words may be difficult for you to speak. It may not be your primary love language. It may take great effort for you to learn this second language. That will be especially true if you have a pattern of critical and condemning words, but I can assure you that it will be worth the effort.

Kind Words

Love is kind. If then we are to communicate love verbally, we must use kind words. That has to do with the way we speak. The same sentence can have two different meanings, depending on how you say it. The statement "I love you," when said with kindness and tenderness, can be a genuine expression of love. But what about the statement "I love you?" The question mark changes the whole meaning of those three words. Sometimes our words are saying one thing, but our tone of voice is saying another. We are sending double messages. Our spouse will usually interpret our message based on our tone of voice, not the words we use.

"I would be delighted to wash dishes tonight," said in a snarling tone will not be received as an expression of love. On the other hand, we can share hurt, pain, and even anger in a kind manner, and that will be an expression of love. "I felt disappointed and hurt that you didn't offer to help me this evening," said in an honest, kind manner, can be an expression of love. The person speaking wants to be known by her spouse. She is taking steps to build intimacy by sharing her feelings. She is asking for an opportunity to discuss a hurt in order to find healing. The same words expressed with a loud, harsh voice will be not an expression of love but an expression of condemnation and judgment.

The manner in which we speak is exceedingly important. An ancient sage once said, "A soft answer turns away anger." When your spouse is angry and upset and lashing out words of heat, if you choose to be loving you will not reciprocate with additional heat but with a soft voice. You will receive what he is saying as information about his emotional feelings. You will let him tell you of his hurt, anger, and perception of events. You will seek to put yourself in his shoes and see the event through his eyes and then express softly and kindly your understanding of why he feels that way. If you have wronged him, you will be willing to confess the wrong and ask forgiveness. If your motivation is different from what he is reading, you will be able to explain your motivation kindly. You will seek understanding and reconciliation, and not to prove your own perception as the only logical way to interpret what has happened. That is mature love—love to which we aspire if we seek a growing marriage.

Love doesn't keep a score of wrongs. Love doesn't bring up past failures. None of us is perfect. In marriage we do not always do the best or right thing. We have sometimes done and said hurtful things to our spouses. We cannot erase the past. We can only confess it and agree that it was wrong. We can ask for forgiveness and try to act differently in the future. Having confessed my failure and asked forgiveness, I can do nothing more to mitigate the hurt it may have caused my spouse. When I have been wronged by my spouse and she has painfully confessed it and requested forgiveness, I have the option of justice or forgiveness. If I choose justice and seek to pay her back or make her pay for her wrongdoing, I am making myself the judge and her the felon. Intimacy becomes impossible. If, however, I choose to forgive, intimacy can be restored. Forgiveness is the way of love.

I am amazed by how many individuals mess up every new day with yesterday. They insist on bringing into today the failures of yesterday and in so doing, they pollute a potentially wonderful day. "I can't believe you did it. I don't think I'll ever forget it. You can't possibly know how much you hurt me. I don't know how you can sit there so smugly after you treated me that way. You ought to be crawling on your knees, begging me for forgiveness. I don't know if I can ever forgive you." Those are not the words of love but of bitterness and resentment and revenge.

The best thing we can do with the failures of the past is to let them be history. Yes, it happened. Certainly it hurt. And it may still hurt, but he has acknowledged his failure and asked your forgiveness. We cannot erase the past, but we can accept it as history. We can choose to live today free from the failures of yesterday. Forgiveness is not a feeling; it is a commitment. It is a choice to show mercy, not to hold the offense up against the offender. Forgiveness is an expression of love. "I love you. I care about you, and I choose to forgive you. Even though my feelings of hurt may linger, I will not allow what has happened to come between us. I hope that we can learn from this experience. You are not a failure because you have failed. You are my spouse, and together we will go on from here." Those are the words of affirmation expressed in the dialect of kind words.

Humble Words

Love makes requests, not demands. When I demand things from my spouse, I become a parent and she the child. It is the parent who tells the three-year-old what he ought to do and, in fact, what he must do. That is necessary because the three-year-old does not yet know how to navigate in the treacherous waters of life. In marriage, however, we are equal, adult partners. We are not perfect to be sure, but we are adults and we are partners. If we are to develop an intimate relationship, we need to know each other's desires. If we wish to love each other, we need to know what the other person wants.

The way we express those desires, however, is all-important. If they come across as demands, we have erased the possibility of intimacy and will drive our spouse away. If, however, we make known our needs and desires as requests, we are giving guidance, not ultimatums. The husband who says, "You know those apple pies you make? Would it be possible for you to make one this week? I love those apple pies," is giving his wife guidance on how to love him and thus build intimacy. On the other hand, the husband who says, "Haven't had an apple pie since the baby was born. Don't guess I'll get any more apple pies for eighteen years," has ceased being an adult and has reverted to adolescent behavior. Such demands do not build intimacy. The wife who says, "Do you think it will be possible for you to clean the gutters this weekend?" is expressing love by making a request. But the wife who says, "If you don't get those gutters cleaned out soon, they are going to fall off the house. They already have trees growing out of them!" has ceased to love and has become a domineering spouse.

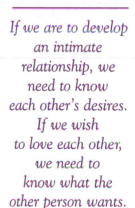

If we are to develop an intimate relationship, we need to know each other's desires. If we wish to love each other, we need to know what the other person wants.

When you make a request of your spouse, you are affirming his or her worth and abilities. You are in essence indicating that she has something or can do something that is meaningful and worthwhile to you. When, however, you make demands, you have become not a lover but a tyrant. Your spouse will feel not affirmed but belittled. A request introduces the element of choice. Your mate may choose to respond to your request or to deny it, because love is always a choice. That's what makes it meaningful. To know that my spouse loves me enough to respond to one of my requests communicates emotionally that she cares about me, respects me, admires me, and wants to do something to please me. We cannot get emotional love by way of demand. My spouse may in fact comply with my demands, but it is not an expression of love. It is an act of fear or guilt or some other emotion, but not love. Thus, a request creates the possibility for an expression of love, whereas a demand suffocates that possibility.

Various Dialects

Words of affirmation are one of the five basic love languages. Within that language, however, there are many dialects. We have discussed a few already, and there are many more. Entire volumes and numerous articles have been written on these dialects. All of the dialects have in common the use of words to affirm one's spouse. Psychologist William James said that possibly the deepest human need is the need to feel appreciated. Words of affirmation will meet that need in many individuals. If you are not a man or woman of words, if it is not your primary love language but you think it may be the love language of your spouse, let me suggest that you keep a notebook titled "Words of Affirmation." When you read an article or book on love, record the words of affirmation you find. When you hear a lecture on love or you overhear a friend saying something positive about another person, write it down. In time, you will collect quite a list of words to use in communicating love to your spouse.

You may also want to try giving indirect words of affirmation, that is, saying positive things about your spouse when he or she is not present. Eventually, someone will tell your spouse, and you will get full credit for love. Tell your wife's mother how great your wife is. When her mother tells her what you said, it will be amplified, and you will get even more credit. Also affirm your spouse in front of others when he or she is present. When you are given public honor for an accomplishment, be sure to share the credit with your spouse. You may also try your hand at writing words of affirmation. Written words have the benefit of being read over and over again.

I learned an important lesson about words of affirmation and love languages in Little Rock, Arkansas. My visit with Bill and Betty Jo was on a beautiful spring day. They lived in a cluster home with white picket fence, green grass, and spring flowers in full bloom. It was idyllic. Once inside, however, I discovered that the idealism ended. Their marriage was in shambles. Twelve years and two children after the wedding day, they wondered why they had married in the first place. They seemed to disagree on everything. The only thing they really agreed on was that they both loved the children. As the story unraveled, my observation was that Bill was a workaholic who had little time left over for Betty Jo. Betty Jo worked part-time, mainly to get out of the house. Their method of coping was withdrawal. They tried to put distance between themselves so that their conflicts would not seem as large. But the gauge on both love tanks read "empty."

They told me that they had been going for marriage counseling but didn't seem to be making much progress. They were attending my marriage seminar, and I was leaving town the next day. This would likely be my only encounter with Bill and Betty Jo. I decided to put all my eggs in one basket.

I spent an hour with each of them separately. I listened intently to both stories. I discovered that in spite of the emptiness of their relationship and their many disagreements, they appreciated certain things about each other. Bill acknowledged, "She is a good mother. She also is a good housekeeper and an excellent cook when she chooses to cook. But," he continued, "there is simply no affection coming from her. I work my butt off and there is simply no appreciation." In my conversation with Betty Jo, she agreed that Bill was an excellent provider. "But," she complained, "he does nothing around the house to help me, and he never has time for me. What's the use of having the house, the recreational vehicle, and all the other things if you don't ever get to enjoy them together?"

With that information, I decided to focus my advice by making only one suggestion to each of them. I told Bill and Betty Jo separately that each one held the key to changing the emotional climate of the marriage. "That key," I said, "is to express verbal appreciation for the things you like about the other person and, for the moment, suspending your complaints about the things you do not like." We reviewed the positive comments they had already made about each other and helped each of them write a list of those positive traits. Bill's list focused on Betty Jo's activities as a mother, housekeeper, and cook. Betty Jo's list focused on Bill's hard work and financial provision of the family. We made the lists as specific as possible. Betty Jo's list looked like this:

- He hasn't missed a day of work in twelve years.
  He is aggressive in his work.

- He has received several promotions through the years.
  He is always thinking of ways to improve his productivity.

- He makes the house payment each month.

- He also pays the electrical bill, the gas bill, the water bill.

- He bought us a recreational vehicle three years ago.

- He mows the grass or hires someone to do it each week
  in the spring and summer.

- He rakes the leaves or hires someone to do it in the fall.

- He provides plenty of money for food and clothing for
  the family.

- He carries the garbage out about once a month.

- He provides money for me to buy Christmas presents
  for the family.

- He agrees that I can use the money I make at my part-time job any way I desire.

Bill's list looked like this:

- She makes the beds every day.

- She vacuums the house every week.

- She gets the kids off to school every morning with a good breakfast.

- She cooks dinner about three days a week.

- She buys the groceries.

- She helps the children with their homework.

- She transports the children to school and church activities.

- She teaches first grade Sunday school.

- She takes my clothes to the cleaners.

- She does the washing and some ironing.

I suggested that they add to the lists things they noticed in the weeks ahead. I also suggested that twice a week, they select one positive trait and express verbal appreciation for it to the spouse. I gave one further guideline. I told Betty Jo that if Bill happened to give her a compliment, she was not to give him a compliment at the same time but rather, she should simply receive it and say, "Thank you for saying that." I told Bill the same thing. I encouraged them to do that every week for two months, and if they found it helpful, they could continue. If the experiment did not help the emotional climate of the marriage, then they could write it off as another failed attempt.

The next day, I got on the plane and returned home. I made a note to call Bill and Betty Jo two months later to see what had happened. When I called them in mid-summer, I asked to speak to each of them individually. I was amazed to find that Bill's attitude had taken a giant step forward. He had guessed that I had given Betty Jo the same advice I had given him, but that was all right. He loved it. She was expressing appreciation for his hard work and his provision for the family. "She has actually made me feel like a man again. We've got a ways to go, Dr. Chapman, but I really believe we are on the road."

When I talked to Betty Jo, however, I found that she had only taken a baby step forward. She said, "It has improved some, Dr. Chapman. Bill is giving me verbal compliments as you suggested, and I guess he is sincere. But, Dr. Chapman, he's still not spending any time with me. He is still so busy at work that we never have time together."

As I listened to Betty Jo, the lights came on. I knew that I had made a significant discovery. The love language of one person is not necessarily the love language of another. It was obvious that Bill's primary love language was words of affirmation. He was a hard worker, and he enjoyed his work, but what he wanted most from his wife was expressions of appreciation for his work. That pattern was probably set in childhood, and the need for verbal affirmation was no less important in his adult life. Betty Jo, on the other hand, was emotionally crying out for something else. Positive words were fine, but her deep emotional longing is for something else. That brings us to love language number two.

NOTES
1. Proverbs 18:21.
2. Proverbs 12:25.

If your spouse's love language is *Words of Affirmation:*

1. To remind yourself that "Words of Affirmation" is your spouse's primary love language, print the following on a 3x5 card and put it on a mirror or other place where you will see it daily:

   Words are important!
   Words are important!
   Words are important!

2. For one week, keep a written record of all the words of affirmation you give your spouse each day. At the end of the week, sit down with your spouse and review your record.

   On Monday, I said:
   "You did a great job on this meal."
   "You really look nice in that outfit."
   "I really appreciate your picking up the laundry."

   On Tuesday, I said:
   etc.

   You might be surprised how well (or how poorly) you are speaking words of affirmation.

3. Set a goal to give your spouse a different compliment each day for one month. If "an apple a day keeps the doctor away," maybe a compliment a day will keep the counselor away. (You may want to record these compliments also, so you will not duplicate the statements.)

4. As you read the newspaper, magazines, and books, or watch TV or listen to radio, look for words of affirmation which people use. Observe people in conversation. Write those affirming statements in a notebook. (If they are cartoons, clip and paste

them in your notebook.) Read through these periodically and select those you could use with your spouse. When you use one, note the date on which you used it. Your notebook may become your love book. Remember, words are important!

5. Write a love letter, a love paragraph, or a love sentence to your spouse, and give it quietly or with fanfare! (Chances are, when he dies, you will find your love letter tucked away in some special place.) Words are important!

6. Compliment your spouse in the presence of his parents or friends. You will get double credit: Your spouse will feel loved and the parents will feel lucky to have such a great son-in-law or daughter-in-law.

7. Look for your spouse's strengths and tell her how much you appreciate those strengths. Chances are she will work hard to live up to her reputation.

8. Tell your children how great their mother or father is. Do this behind your spouse's back and in her presence.

9. Write a poem describing how you feel about your spouse. If you are not a poet, choose a card that expresses how you feel. Underline special words and add a few of your own at the end.

10. If you find speaking "Words of Affirmation" is difficult for you, practice in front of a mirror. Use a cue card if you must, and remember, words are important.

THE FIVE LOVE LANGUAGES

Words of Affirmation

QUALITY TIME

Receiving Gifts

Acts of Service

Physical Touch

LOVE LANGUAGE #2: *Quality Time*

I should have picked up on Betty Jo's primary love language from the beginning. What was she saying on that spring night when I visited her and Bill in Little Rock? "Bill is a good provider, but he doesn't spend any time with me. What good is the house and the recreational vehicle and all the other things if we don't ever enjoy them together?" What was her desire? Quality time with Bill. She wanted his attention. She wanted him to focus on her, to give her time, to do things with her.

By "quality time," I mean giving someone your undivided attention. I don't mean sitting on the couch watching television together. When you spend time that way, ABC or NBC has your attention—not your spouse. What I mean is sitting on the couch with the TV off, looking at each other and *talking,* giving each other your undivided attention. It means taking a walk, just the two of you, or going out to eat and looking at each other and talking. Have you ever noticed that in a restaurant, you can almost always tell the difference between a dating couple and a married couple? Dating couples look at each other and talk. Married couples sit there and gaze around the restaurant. You'd think they went there to eat!

THE DAFFODIL:
"The sun shines when I'm with you."

When I sit on the couch with my wife and give her twenty minutes of my undivided attention and she does the same for me, we are giving each other twenty minutes of life. We will never have those twenty minutes again; we are giving our lives to each other. It is a powerful emotional communicator of love.

One medicine cannot cure all diseases. In my advice to Bill and Betty Jo, I made a serious mistake. I assumed that words of affirmation would mean as much to Betty Jo as they would to Bill. I had hoped that if each of them would give adequate verbal affirmation, the emotional climate would change, and both of them would begin to feel loved. It worked for Bill. He began to feel more positive about Betty Jo. He began to sense genuine appreciation for his hard work, but it had not worked as well for Betty Jo, for words of affirmation were not her primary love language. Her language was quality time.

I got back on the phone and thanked Bill for his efforts in the past two months. I told him that he had done a good job of verbally affirming Betty Jo and that she had heard his affirmations. "But, Dr. Chapman," he said, "she is still not very happy. I don't think things are much better for her."

"You are right," I said, "and I think I know why. The problem is that I suggested the wrong love language." Bill hadn't the foggiest idea what I meant. I explained that what makes one person feel loved emotionally is not always the thing that makes another person feel loved emotionally.

He agreed that his language was words of affirmation. He told me how much that had meant to him as a boy and how good he felt when Betty Jo expressed appreciation for the things he did. I explained that Betty Jo's language was not words of affirmation but quality time. I explained the concept of giving someone your undivided attention, not talking to her while you read the newspaper or watch television but looking into her eyes, giving her your full attention, doing something with her that she enjoys doing and doing it wholeheartedly. "Like going to the symphony with her," he said. I could tell the lights were coming on in Little Rock.

"Dr. Chapman, that is what she has always complained about. I didn't do things with her, I didn't spend any time with her. 'We used to go places and do things before we were married,' she said, 'but now, you're too busy.' That's her love language all right; no question about it. But, Dr. Chapman, what am I gonna do? My job is so demanding."

"Tell me about it," I said.

For the next ten minutes, he gave me the history of his climb up the organizational ladder, of how hard he had worked, and how proud he was of his accomplishments. He told me of his dreams for the future and that he knew that within the next five years, he would be where he wanted to be.

"Do you want to be there alone, or do you want to be there with Betty Jo and the children?" I asked.

"I want her to be with me, Dr. Chapman. I want her to enjoy it with me. That's why it always hurts so much when she criticizes me for spending time on the job. I am doing it for us. I wanted her to be a part of it, but she is always so negative."

"Are you beginning to see why she was so negative, Bill?" I asked. "Her love language is quality time. You have given her so little time that her love tank is empty. She doesn't feel secure in your love. Therefore she has lashed out at what was taking your time in her mind— your job. She doesn't really hate your job. She hates the fact that she feels so little love coming from you. There's only one answer, Bill, and it's costly. You have to make time for Betty Jo. You have to love her in the right love language."

"I know you are right, Dr. Chapman. Where do I begin?"

"Do you have your legal pad handy? The one on which we made the list of the positive things about Betty Jo?"

"It's right here."

"Good. We're going to make another list. What are some things that you know Betty Jo would like you to do with her? Things she has mentioned through the years." Here is Bill's list:

- Take our RV and spend a weekend in the mountains (sometimes with the children and sometimes just the two of us).

- Meet her for lunch (at a nice restaurant or sometimes even at McDonald's).

- Get a baby-sitter and take her out to dinner, just the two of us.

- When I come home at night, sit down and talk with her about my day and listen as she tells me about her day. (She doesn't want me to watch TV while we are trying to talk.)

- Spend time talking with the children about their school experiences.

- Spend time playing games with the children.

- Go on a picnic with her and the children on Saturday and don't complain about the ants and the flies.

- Take a vacation with the family at least once a year.

- Go walking with her and talk as we walk. (Don't walk ahead of her.)

"Those are the things she has talked about through the years," he said.

"You know what I am going to suggest, don't you, Bill?"

"Do them," he said.

"That's right, one a week for the next two months. Where will you find the time? You will make it. You are a wise man," I continued. "You would not be where you are if you were not a good decision maker. You have the ability to plan your life and to include Betty Jo in your plans."

"I know," he said, "I can do it."

"And, Bill, this does not have to diminish your vocational goals. It just means that when you get to the top, Betty Jo and the children will be with you."

"That's what I want more than anything. Whether I am at the top or not, I want her to be happy, and I want to enjoy life with her and the children."

The years have come and gone. Bill and Betty Jo have gone to the top and back, but the important thing is that they have done it together. The children have left the nest, and Bill and Betty Jo agree that these are their best years ever. Bill has become an avid symphony fan, and Betty Jo has made an unending list in her legal pad of things she appreciates about Bill. He never tires of hearing them. He has now started his own company and is near the top again. His job is no longer a threat to Betty Jo. She is excited about it and encourages him. She knows that she is number one in his life. Her love tank is full, and if it begins to get empty, she knows that a simple request on her part will get her Bill's undivided attention.

Togetherness

A central aspect of quality time is togetherness. I do not mean proximity. Two people sitting in the same room are in close proximity, but they are not necessarily together. Togetherness has to do with focused attention. When a father is sitting on the floor, rolling a ball to his two-year-old, his attention is not focused on the ball but on his child. For that brief moment, however long it lasts, they are together. If, however, the father is talking on the phone while he rolls the ball, his attention is diluted. Some husbands and wives think they are spending time together when, in reality, they are only living in close proximity. They are in the same house at the same time, but they are not together. A husband who is watching sports on television while

A central aspect of quality time is togetherness. I do not mean proximity. . . . Togetherness has to do with focused attention.

he talks to his wife is not giving her quality time, because she does not have his full attention.

Quality time does not mean that we have to spend our together moments gazing into each other's eyes. It means that we are doing something together and that we are giving our full attention to the other person. The activity in which we are both engaged is incidental.

The important thing emotionally is that we are spending focused time with each other. The activity is a vehicle that creates the sense of togetherness. The important thing about the father rolling the ball to the two-year-old is not the activity itself, but the emotions that are created between the father and his child.

Similarly, a husband and wife playing tennis together, if it is genuine quality time, will focus not on the game but on the fact that they are spending time together. What happens on the emotional level is what matters. Our spending time together in a common pursuit communicates that we care about each other, that we enjoy being with each other, that we like to do things together.

Quality Conversation

Like words of affirmation, the language of quality time also has many dialects. One of the most common dialects is that of quality conversation. By quality conversation, I mean sympathetic dialogue where two individuals are sharing their experiences, thoughts, feelings, and desires in a friendly, uninterrupted context. Most individuals who complain that their spouse does not talk do not mean literally that he or she never says a word. They mean that he or she seldom takes part in sympathetic dialogue. If your spouse's primary love language is quality time, such dialogue is crucial to his or her emotional sense of being loved.

Quality conversation is quite different from the first love language. Words of affirmation focus on what we are *saying*, whereas quality conversation focuses on what we are *hearing*. If I am sharing my love for you by means of quality time and we are going to spend that time in conversation, it means I will focus on drawing you out, listening sympathetically to what you have to say. I will ask questions, not in a badgering manner but with a genuine desire to understand your thoughts, feelings, and desires.

I met Patrick when he was forty-three and had been married for seventeen years. I remember him because his first words were so dramatic. He sat in the leather chair in my office and after briefly introducing himself, he leaned forward and said with great emotion, "Dr. Chapman, I have been a fool, a real fool."

"What has led you to that conclusion?" I asked.

"I've been married for seventeen years," he said, "and my wife has left me. Now I realize what a fool I've been."

I repeated my original question, "In what way have you been a fool?"

"My wife would come home from work and tell me about the problems in her office. I would listen to her and then tell her what I thought she should do. I always gave her advice. I told her she had to confront the problem. 'Problems don't go away. You have to talk with the people involved or your supervisor. You have to deal with problems.' The next day she would come home from work and tell me about the same problems. I would ask her if she did what I had suggested the day before. She would shake her head and say no. So I'd repeat my advice. I told her that was the way to deal with the situation. She would come home the next day and tell me about the same problems. Again I would ask her if she had done what I had suggested. She would shake her head and say no.

"After three or four nights of that, I would get angry. I would tell her not to expect any sympathy from me if she wasn't willing to take the advice I was giving her. She didn't have to live under that kind of stress and pressure. She could solve the problem if she would simply do what I told her. It hurt me to see her living under such stress because I knew she didn't have to. The next time she'd bring up the problem, I would say, 'I don't want to hear about it. I've told you what you need to do. If you're not going to listen to my advice, I don't want to hear it.'

Many of us . . . are trained to analyze problems and create solutions. We forget that marriage is a relationship, not a project to be completed or a problem to solve.

"I would withdraw and go about my business. What a fool I was," he said, "what a fool! Now I realize that she didn't want advice when she told me about her struggles at work. She wanted sympathy. She wanted me to listen, to give her attention, to let her know that I could understand the hurt, the stress, the pressure. She wanted to know that I loved her and that I was with her. She didn't want advice; she just wanted to know that I understood. But I never tried to understand. I was too busy giving advice. What a fool. And now she is gone. Why can't you see these things when you are going through them?" he asked. "I was blind to what was going on. Only now do I understand how I failed her."

Patrick's wife had been pleading for quality conversation. Emotionally, she longed for him to focus attention on her by listening to her pain and frustration. Patrick was not focusing on listening but on speaking. He listened only long enough to hear the problem and formulate a solution. He didn't listen long enough or well enough to hear her cry for support and understanding.

Many of us are like Patrick. We are trained to analyze problems and create solutions. We forget that marriage is a relationship, not a project to be completed or a problem to solve. A relationship calls for sympathetic listening with a view to understanding the other person's thoughts, feelings, and desires. We must be willing to give advice but only when it is requested and never in a condescending manner. Most of us have little training in listening. We are far more efficient in thinking and speaking. Learning to listen may be as difficult as learning a foreign language, but learn we must, if we want to communicate love. That is especially true if your spouse's primary love language is quality time and his or her dialect is quality conversation. Fortunately, numerous books and articles have been written on developing the art of listening. I will not seek to repeat what is written elsewhere but suggest the following summary of practical tips.

1. *Maintain eye contact when your spouse is talking.* That keeps your mind from wandering and communicates that he/she has your full attention.

2. *Don't listen to your spouse and do something else at the same time.* Remember, quality time is giving someone your undivided attention. If you are watching, reading, or doing something else in which you are keenly interested and cannot turn from immediately, tell your spouse the truth. A positive approach might be, "I know you are trying to talk to me and I'm interested, but I want to give you my full attention. I can't do that right now, but if you will give me ten minutes to finish this, I'll sit down and listen to you." Most spouses will respect such a request.

3. *Listen for feelings.* Ask yourself, "What emotion is my spouse experiencing?" When you think you have the answer, confirm it. For example, "It sounds to me like you are feeling disappointed because I forgot _____." That gives him the chance to clarify his feelings. It also communicates that you are listening intently to what he is saying.

4. *Observe body language.* Clenched fists, trembling hands, tears, furrowed brows, and eye movement may give you clues as to what the other is feeling. Sometimes body language speaks one message while words speak another. Ask for clarification to make sure you know what she is really thinking and feeling.

5. *Refuse to interrupt.* Recent research has indicated that the average individual listens for only seventeen seconds before interrupting and interjecting his own ideas. If I give you my undivided attention while you are talking, I will refrain from

defending myself or hurling accusations at you or dogmatically stating my position. My goal is to discover your thoughts and feelings. My objective is not to defend myself or to set you straight. It is to understand you.

Learning to Talk

Quality conversation requires not only sympathetic listening but also self-revelation. When a wife says, "I wish my husband would talk. I never know what he's thinking or feeling," she is pleading for intimacy. She wants to feel close to her husband, but how can she feel close to someone whom she doesn't know? In order for her to feel loved, he must learn to reveal himself. If her primary love language is quality time and her dialect is quality conversation, her emotional love tank will never be filled until he tells her his thoughts and feelings.

Self-revelation does not come easy for some of us. Many adults grew up in homes where the expression of thoughts and feelings was not encouraged but condemned. To request a toy was to receive a lecture on the sad state of family finances. The child went away feeling guilty for having the desire, and he quickly learned not to express his desires. When he expressed anger, the parents responded with harsh and condemning words. Thus, the child learned that expressing angry feelings is not appropriate. If the child was made to feel guilty for expressing disappointment at not being able to go to the store with his father, he learned to hold his disappointment inside. By the time we reach adulthood, many of us have learned to deny our feelings. We are no longer in touch with our emotional selves.

A wife says to her husband, "How did you feel about what Don did?" And the husband responds, "I think he was wrong. He should have—" but he is not telling her his feelings. He is voicing his thoughts. Perhaps he has reason to feel angry, hurt, or disappointed, but he has lived so long in the world of thought that he does not acknowledge his feelings. When he decides to learn the language of quality conversation, it will be like learning a foreign language. The place to begin is by getting in touch with his feelings, becoming aware that he is an emotional creature in spite of the fact that he has denied that part of his life.

If you need to learn the language of quality conversation, begin by noting the emotions you feel away from home. Carry a small notepad and keep it with you daily. Three times each day, ask yourself, "What emotions have I felt in the last three hours? What did I feel on the way to work when the driver behind me was riding my bumper? What did I feel when I stopped at the gas station and the automatic pump did not shut off and the side of the car was covered with gas? What did I feel when I got to the office and found that my secretary had been assigned to a special work project for the morning? What did I feel when my supervisor told me that the project I was working on had to be completed in three days when I thought I had another two weeks?"

Write down your feelings in the notepad and a word or two to help you remember the event corresponding to the feeling. Your list may look like this:

If you need to learn the language of quality conversation, begin by noting the emotions you feel away from home.

EVENT	FEELINGS
• tailgater	• angry
• gas station	• very upset
• no secretary	• disappointed
• work project due in three days	• frustrated and anxious

Do that exercise three times a day, and you will develop an awareness of your emotional nature. Using your notepad, communicate your emotions and the events briefly with your spouse as many days as possible. In a few weeks, you will become comfortable expressing your emotions with him or her. And eventually you will feel comfortable discussing your emotions toward your spouse, the children, and events that occur within the home. Remember, emotions themselves are neither good nor bad. They are simply our psychological responses to the events of life.

Based on our thoughts and emotions, we eventually make decisions. When the tailgater was following you on the highway and you felt angry, perhaps you had these thoughts: *I wish he would lay off; I wish he would pass me; if I thought I wouldn't get caught, I'd press the accelerator and leave him in the twilight; I should slam on my brakes and let his insurance company buy me a new car; maybe I'll pull off the road and let him pass.*

Eventually, you made some decision or the other driver backed off, turned, or passed you, and you arrived safely at work. In each of life's events, we have emotions, thoughts, desires, and eventually actions. It is the expression of that process that we call self-revelation. If you choose to learn the love dialect of quality conversation, that is the learning road you must follow.

Personality Types

Not all of us are out of touch with our emotions, but when it comes to talking, all of us are affected by our personality. I have observed two basic personality types. The first I call the "Dead Sea." In the little nation of Israel, the Sea of Galilee flows south by way of the Jordan River into the Dead Sea. The Dead Sea goes nowhere. It receives but it does not give. This personality type receives many experiences, emotions, and thoughts throughout the day. They have a large reservoir where they store that information, and they are perfectly happy not to talk. If you say to a Dead Sea personality, "What's wrong? Why aren't you talking tonight?" he will probably answer, "Nothing's wrong. What makes you think something's wrong?" And that response is perfectly honest. He is content not to talk. He could drive from Chicago to Detroit and never say a word and be perfectly happy.

On the other extreme is the "Babbling Brook." For this personality, whatever enters into the eye gate or the ear gate comes out the mouth gate and there are seldom sixty seconds between the two. Whatever they see, whatever they hear, they tell. In fact if no one is at home to talk to, they will call someone else. "Do you know what I saw? Do you know what I heard?" If they can't get someone on the telephone, they may talk to themselves because they have no reservoir. Many times a Dead Sea marries a Babbling Brook. That happens because when they are dating, it is a very attractive match.

If you are a Dead Sea and you date a Babbling Brook, you will have a wonderful evening. You don't have to think, "How will I get the conversation started tonight? How will I keep the conversation flowing?" In fact, you don't have to think at all. All you have to do is nod your head and say, "Uh-huh," and she will fill up the whole evening and you will go home saying, "What a wonderful person." On the other hand, if you are a Babbling Brook and you date a Dead Sea, you will have an equally wonderful evening because Dead Seas are the world's best listeners. You will babble for three hours. He will listen intently to you, and you will go home saying, "What a wonderful person." You attract each other. But five years after marriage, the Babbling Brook wakes up one morning and says, "We've been married five years, and I don't know him." The Dead Sea is saying, "I know her *too* well. I wish she would stop the flow and give me a break." The good news is that Dead Seas can learn to talk and Babbling Brooks can learn to listen. We are influenced by our personality but not controlled by it.

One way to learn new patterns is to establish a daily sharing time in which each of you will talk about three things that happened to you that day and how you feel about them.

One way to learn new patterns is to establish a daily sharing time in which each of you will talk about three things that happened to you that day and how you feel about them. I call that the "Minimum Daily Requirement" for a healthy marriage. If you will start with the daily minimum, in a few weeks or months you may find quality conversation flowing more freely between you.

Quality Activities

In addition to the basic love language of quality time, or giving your spouse your undivided attention, is another dialect called quality activities. At a recent marriage seminar, I asked couples to complete the following sentence: "I feel most loved by my husband/wife when _____." Here is the response of a twenty-nine-year-old husband who has been married for eight years: "I feel most loved by my wife when we do things together, things I like to do and things she likes to do. We talk more. It sorta feels like we are dating again." That is a typical response of individuals whose primary love language is quality time. The emphasis is on being together, doing things together, giving each other undivided attention.

Quality activities may include anything in which one or both of you have an interest. The emphasis is not on what you are doing but on why you are doing it. The purpose is to experience something together, to walk away from it feeling "He cares about me. He was willing to do something with me that I enjoy, and he did it with a positive attitude." That is love, and for some people it is love's loudest voice.

Tracie grew up with the symphony. Throughout her childhood, the house was filled with classical music. At least once a year, she accompanied her parents to the symphony. Larry, on the other hand, grew up on country and western music. He never actually attended a concert, but the radio was always on, tuned to the country station. The symphony he called elevator music. Had he not married Tracie, he could have lived his life without ever attending the symphony. Before they were married, while he was still in the obsessed state of being in love, he went to the symphony. But even in his euphoric emotional state, his attitude was, "You call this stuff music?" After marriage, that was one experience he never expected to repeat. When, however, he discovered several years later that quality time was Tracie's primary love language and that she especially liked the dialect of quality activities and that attending the symphony was one of those activities, he chose to go with an enthusiastic spirit. His purpose was clear. It was not to attend the symphony but to love Tracie and to speak her language loudly. In time, he did come to appreciate the symphony and even occasionally to enjoy a movement or two. He may never become a symphony lover, but he has become proficient at loving Tracie.

Quality activities may include such activities as putting in a garden, visiting flea markets, shopping for antiques, listening to music, picnicking together, taking long walks, or washing the car together on a hot summer day. The activities are limited only by your interest and willingness to try new experiences. The essential ingredients in a quality activity are: (1) at least one of you wants to do it, (2) the other is willing to do it, (3) both of you know why you are doing it—to express love by being together.

One of the by-products of quality activities is that they provide a memory bank from which to draw in the years ahead. Fortunate is the couple who remembers an early morning stroll along the coast, the spring they planted the flower garden, the time they got poison ivy chasing the rabbit through the woods, the night they attended their first major league baseball game together, the one and only time they went skiing together and he broke his leg, the amusement parks, the concerts, the cathedrals, and oh, yes, the awe of standing beneath the waterfall after the two-mile hike. They can almost feel the mist as they remember. Those are memories of love, especially for the person whose primary love language is quality time.

One of the by-products of quality activities is that they provide a memory bank from which to draw in the years ahead.

And where do we find time for such activities, especially if both of us have vocations outside the home? We make time just as we make time for lunch and dinner. Why? Because it is just as essential to our marriage as meals are to our health. Is it difficult? Does it take careful planning? Yes. Does it mean we have to give up some individual activities? Perhaps. Does it mean we do some things we don't particularly enjoy? Certainly. Is it worth it? Without a doubt. What's in it for me? The pleasure of living with a spouse who feels loved and knowing that I have learned to speak his or her love language fluently.

A personal word of thanks to Bill and Betty Jo in Little Rock, who taught me the value of love language number one, words of affirmation, and love language number two, quality time. Now, it's on to Chicago and love language number three.

If your spouse's love language is *Quality Time:*

1. Take a walk together through the old neighborhood where one of you grew up. Ask questions about your spouse's childhood. Ask, "What are the fun memories of your childhood?" Then, "What was most painful about your childhood?"

2. Go to the city park and rent bicycles. Ride until you are tired, then sit and watch the ducks. When you get tired of the quacks, roll on to the rose garden. Learn each other's favorite color of rose and why. (If the bikes are too much, take turns pulling each other in a little red wagon.)

3. In the spring or summer make a luncheon appointment with your spouse. Meet him and drive to the local cemetery. Spread your tablecloth and eat your sandwiches and thank God that you are still alive. Share with each other one thing you would like to do before you die.

4. Ask your spouse for a list of five activities that he would enjoy doing with you. Make plans to do one of them each month for the next five months. If money is a problem, space the freebies between the "we can't afford this" events.

5. Ask your spouse where she most enjoys sitting when talking with you. The next week, call her one afternoon and say, "I want to make a date with you one evening this week to sit on the yellow sofa and talk. Which night and what time would be best for you?" (Don't say "yellow sofa" if her favorite place is in the Jacuzzi!)

6. Think of an activity your spouse enjoys, but which brings little pleasure to you: football, symphony, jazz concert, or TV sleeping. Tell your spouse that you are trying to broaden your horizons and would like to join her in this activity sometime this month. Set a date and give it your best effort. Ask questions about the activity at break times.

7. Plan a weekend getaway just for the two of you sometime within the next six months. Be sure it is a weekend when you won't have to call the office or turn on the TV for a report every thirty minutes. Focus on relaxing together doing what one or both of you enjoy.

8. Make time every day to share with each other some of the events of the day. When you spend more time watching the news than you do listening to each other, you end up more concerned about Bosnia than about your spouse.

9. Have a "Let's review our history" evening once every three months. Set aside an hour to focus on your history. Select five questions each of you will answer, such as:

   (1) Who was your best and worst teacher in school and why?
   (2) When did you feel your parents were proud of you?
   (3) What is the worst mistake your mother ever made?
   (4) What is the worst mistake your father ever made?
   (5) What do you remember about the religious aspect of your childhood?

   Each evening, agree on your five questions before you begin your sharing. At the end of the five questions, stop and decide upon the five questions you will ask next time.

10. Camp out by the fireplace (or an orange lamp). Spread your blankets and pillows on the floor. Get your Pepsi and popcorn. Pretend the TV is broken and talk like you used to when you were dating. Talk till the sun comes up or something else happens. If the floor gets too hard, go back upstairs and go to bed. You won't forget this evening!

THE FIVE LOVE LANGUAGES

Words of Affirmation

Quality Time

RECEIVING GIFTS

Acts of Service

Physical Touch

LOVE LANGUAGE #3: *Receiving Gifts*

I was in Chicago when I studied anthropology. By means of detailed ethnographies, I visited fascinating peoples all over the world. I went to Central America and studied the advanced cultures of the Mayans and the Aztecs. I crossed the Pacific and studied the tribal peoples of Melanesia and Polynesia. I studied the Eskimos of the northern tundra and the aboriginal Ainus of Japan. I examined the cultural patterns surrounding love and marriage and found that in every culture I studied, gift giving was a part of the love-marriage process.

Anthropologists are enamored by cultural patterns that tend to pervade cultures, and so was I. Could it be that gift giving is a fundamental expression of love that transcends cultural barriers? Is the attitude of love always accompanied by the concept of giving? Those are academic and somewhat philosophical questions, but if the answer is yes, it has profound practical implications for North American couples.

THE PEONY:
"Happy marriage."

I took an anthropology field trip to the island of Dominica. Our purpose was to study the culture of the Carib Indians, and on the trip I met Fred. Fred was not a Carib but a young black man of twenty-eight years. Fred had lost a hand in a fishing-by-dynamite accident. Since the accident, he could not continue his fishing career. He had plenty of available time, and I welcomed his companionship. We spent hours together talking about his culture.

Upon my first visit to Fred's house, he said to me, "Mr. Gary, would you like to have some juice?" to which I responded enthusiastically. He turned to his younger brother and said, "Go get Mr. Gary some juice." His brother turned, walked down the dirt path, climbed a coconut tree, and returned with a green coconut. "Open it," Fred commanded. With three swift movements of the machete, his brother uncorked the coconut, leaving a triangular hole at the top. Fred handed me the coconut and said, "Juice for you." It was green, but I drank it—all of it—because I knew it was a gift of love. I was his friend, and to friends you give juice.

At the end of our weeks together as I prepared to leave that small island, Fred gave me a final token of his love. It was a crooked stick fourteen inches in length which he had taken from the ocean. It was silky smooth from pounding upon the rocks. Fred said that the stick had lived on the shores of Dominica for a long time, and he wanted me to have it as a reminder of the beautiful island. Even today when I look at that stick, I can almost hear the sound of the Caribbean waves, but it is not as much a reminder of Dominica as it is a reminder of love.

A gift is something you can hold in your hand and say, "Look, he was thinking of me," or, "She remembered me." You must be thinking of someone to give him a gift. The gift itself is a symbol of that thought. It doesn't matter whether it costs money. What is important is that you thought of him. And it is not the thought implanted only in the mind that counts, but the thought expressed in actually securing the gift and giving it as the expression of love.

Mothers remember the days their children bring a flower from the yard as a gift. They feel loved, even if it was a flower they didn't want picked. From early years, children are inclined to give gifts to their parents, which may be another indication that gift giving is fundamental to love.

Gifts are visual symbols of love. Most wedding ceremonies include the giving and receiving of rings. The person performing the ceremony says, "These rings are outward and visible signs of an inward and spiritual bond that unites your two hearts in love that has no end." That is not meaningless rhetoric. It is verbalizing a significant truth—symbols have emotional value. Perhaps that is even more graphically displayed near the end of a disintegrating marriage when the husband or wife stops wearing the wedding ring. It is a visual sign that the marriage is in serious trouble. One husband said, "When she threw her wedding rings at me and angrily walked out of the house slamming the door behind her, I knew our marriage was in serious trouble. I didn't pick up her rings for two days. When I finally did, I cried uncontrollably." The rings were a symbol of what should have been, but lying in his hand and not on her finger, they were visual reminders that the marriage was falling apart. The lonely rings stirred deep emotions within the husband.

Visual symbols of love are more important to some people than to others. That's why individuals have different attitudes toward wedding rings. Some never take the ring off after the wedding. Others don't even wear a wedding band. That is another sign that people have different primary love languages. If receiving gifts is my primary love language, I will place great value on the ring you have given me and I will wear it with great pride. I will also be greatly moved emotionally by other gifts that you give through the years. I will see them as expressions of love. Without gifts as visual symbols, I may question your love.

If your spouse's primary love language is receiving gifts, you can become a proficient gift giver. In fact, it is one of the easiest love languages to learn.

Gifts come in all sizes, colors, and shapes. Some are expensive, and others are free. To the individual whose primary love language is receiving gifts, the cost of the gift will matter little, unless it is greatly out of line with what you can afford. If a millionaire gives only one-dollar gifts regularly, the spouse may question whether that is an expression of love, but when family finances are limited, a one-dollar gift may speak a million dollars worth of love.

Gifts may be purchased, found, or made. The husband who stops along the roadside and picks his wife a wildflower has found himself an expression of love, unless, of course, his wife is allergic to wildflowers. For the man who can afford it, you can purchase a beautiful card for less than five dollars. For the man who cannot, you can make one for free. Get the paper out of the trash can where you work, fold it in the middle, take scissors and cut out a heart, write "I love you," and sign your name. Gifts need not be expensive.

But what of the person who says, "I'm not a gift giver. I didn't receive many gifts growing up. I never learned how to select gifts. It doesn't come naturally for me." Congratulations, you have just made the first discovery in becoming a great lover. You and your spouse speak different love languages. Now that you have made that discovery, get on with the business of learning your second language. If your spouse's primary love language is receiving gifts, you can become a proficient gift giver. In fact, it is one of the easiest love languages to learn.

Where do you begin? Make a list of all the gifts your spouse has expressed excitement about receiving through the years. They may be gifts you have given or gifts given by other family members or friends. The list will give you an idea of the kind of gifts your spouse would enjoy receiving. If you have little or no knowledge about selecting the kinds of gifts on your list, recruit the help of family members who know your spouse. In the meantime, select gifts that you feel comfortable purchasing, making, or finding, and give them to your spouse. Don't wait for a special occasion. If receiving gifts is his/her primary love language, almost anything you give will be received as an expression of love. (If she has been critical of your gifts in the past and almost nothing you have given has been acceptable, then receiving gifts is almost certainly not her primary love language.)

Gifts and Money

If you are to become an effective gift giver, you may have to change your attitude about money. Each of us has an individualized perception of the purposes of money, and we have various emotions associated with spending it. Some of us have a spending orientation. We feel good about ourselves when we are spending money. Others have a saving and investing perspective. We feel good about ourselves when we are saving money and investing it wisely.

If you are a spender, you will have little difficulty purchasing gifts for your spouse; but if you are a saver, you will experience emotional resistance to the idea of spending money as an expression of love. You don't purchase things for yourself. Why should you purchase things for your spouse? But that attitude fails to recognize that you are purchasing things for yourself. By saving and investing money you are purchasing self-worth and emotional security. You are caring for your own emotional needs in the way you handle money. What you are not doing is meeting the emotional needs of your spouse. If you discover that your spouse's primary love language is receiving gifts, then perhaps you will understand that purchasing gifts for him or her is the best investment you can make. You are investing in your relationship and filling your spouse's emotional love tank, and with a full love tank, he or she will likely reciprocate emotional love to you in a language you will understand. When both persons' emotional needs are met, your marriage will take on a whole new dimension. Don't worry about your savings. You will always be a saver, but to invest in loving your spouse is to invest in blue-chip stocks.

The Gift of Self

There is an intangible gift that sometimes speaks more loudly than a gift that can be held in one's hand. I call it the gift of self or the gift of presence. Being there when your spouse needs you speaks loudly to the one whose primary love language is receiving gifts. Jan once said to me, "My husband, Don, loves softball more than he loves me."

"Why do you say that?" I inquired.

"On the day our baby was born, he played softball. I was lying in the hospital all afternoon while he played softball," she said.

"Was he there when the baby was born?"

"Oh, yes. He stayed long enough for the baby to be born, but ten minutes afterward, he left to play softball. I was devastated. It was such an important moment in our lives. I wanted us to share it together. I wanted him to be there with me. Don deserted me to play."

That husband may have sent her a dozen roses, but they would not have spoken as loudly as his presence in the hospital room beside her. I could tell that Jan was deeply hurt by that experience. The "baby" was now fifteen years old, and she was talking about the event with all the emotion as though it had happened yesterday. I probed further. "Have you based your conclusion that Don loves softball more than he loves you on this one experience?"

"Oh, no," she said. "On the day of my mother's funeral, he also played softball."

"Did he go to the funeral?"

"Oh, yes. He went to the funeral, but as soon as it was over, he left to play softball. I couldn't believe it. My brothers and sisters came to the house with me, but my husband was playing softball."

Later, I asked Don about those two events. He knew exactly what I was talking about. "I knew she would bring that up," he said. "I was there through all the labor and when the baby was born. I took pictures; I was so happy. I couldn't wait to tell the guys on the team, but my bubble was burst when I got back to the hospital that evening. She was furious with me. I couldn't believe what she was saying. I thought she would be proud of me for telling the team.

"And when her mother died? She probably did not tell you that I took off work a week before she died and spent the whole week at the hospital and at her mother's house doing repairs and helping out. After she died and the funeral was over, I felt I had done all I could do. I needed a breather. I like to play softball, and I knew that would help me relax and relieve some of the stress I'd been under. I thought she would want me to take a break.

"I had done what I thought was important to her, but it wasn't enough. She has never let me forget those two days. She says that I love softball more than I love her. That's ridiculous."

He was a sincere husband who failed to understand the tremendous power of presence. His being there for his wife was more important than anything else in her mind. Physical presence in the time of crisis is the most powerful gift you can give if your spouse's primary love language is receiving gifts. Your body becomes the symbol of your love. Remove the symbol, and the sense of love evaporates. In counseling, Don and Jan worked through the hurts and misunderstandings of the past. Eventually, Jan was able to forgive him, and Don came to understand why his presence was so important to her.

If the physical presence of your spouse is important to you, I urge you to verbalize that to your spouse. Don't expect him to read your mind. If, on the other hand, your spouse says to you, "I really want you to be there with me tonight, tomorrow, this afternoon," take his request seriously. From your perspective, it may not be important; but if you are not responsive to that request, you may be communicating a message you do not intend. A husband once said, "When my mother died, my wife's supervisor said that she could be off two hours for the funeral but she needed to be back in the office for the afternoon. My wife told him that she felt her husband needed her support that day and she would have to be away the entire day.

Physical presence in the time of crisis is the most powerful gift you can give if your spouse's primary love language is receiving gifts.

"The supervisor replied, 'If you are gone all day, you may well lose your job.'

"My wife said, 'My husband is more important than my job.' She spent the day with me. Somehow that day, I felt more loved by her than ever before. I have never forgotten what she did. Incidentally," he said, "she didn't lose her job. Her supervisor soon left, and she was asked to take his job." That wife had spoken the love language of her husband, and he never forgot it.

Almost everything ever written on the subject of love indicates that at the heart of love is the spirit of giving. All five love languages challenge us to give to our spouse, but for some, receiving gifts, visible symbols of love, speaks the loudest. I heard the most graphic illustration of that truth in Chicago, where I met Jim and Janice.

They attended my marriage seminar and agreed to take me to O'Hare Airport after the seminar on Saturday afternoon. We had two or three hours before my flight, and they asked if I would like to stop at a restaurant. I was famished, so I readily agreed. That afternoon, however, I got much more than a free meal.

Jim and Janice both grew up on farms in central Illinois not more than a hundred miles from each other. They moved to Chicago shortly after their wedding. I was hearing their story fifteen years and three children later. Janice began talking almost immediately after we sat down. She said, "Dr. Chapman, the reason we wanted to take you to the airport is so that we could tell you about our miracle." Something about the word *miracle* always causes me to brace myself, especially if I don't know the person who is using it. *What bizarre story am I going to hear?* I wondered, but I kept my thoughts to myself and gave Janice my undivided attention. I was about to be shocked.

She said, "Dr. Chapman, God used you to perform a miracle in our marriage." I felt guilty already. A moment ago, I was questioning her use of the term *miracle,* and now in her mind I was the vehicle of a miracle. Now I was listening even more intently. Janice continued, "Three years ago, we attended your marriage seminar here in Chicago for the first time. I was desperate," she said. "I was thinking seriously of leaving Jim and had told him so. Our marriage had been empty for a long time. I had given up. For years, I had complained to Jim that I needed his love, but he never responded. I loved the children, and I knew they loved me, but I felt nothing coming from Jim. In fact, by that time, I hated him. He was a methodical person. He did everything by routine. He was as predictable as a clock, and no one could break into his routine.

"For years," she continued, "I tried to be a good wife. I cooked, I washed, I ironed, I cooked, I washed, I ironed. I did all the things I thought a good wife should do. I had sex with him because I knew that was important to him, but I felt no love coming from him. I felt like he stopped dating me after we got married and simply took me for granted. I felt used and unappreciated.

"When I talked to Jim about my feelings, he'd laugh at me and say we had as good a marriage as anybody else in the community. He didn't understand why I was so unhappy. He would remind me that the bills were paid, that we had a nice house and a new car, that I was free to work or not work outside the home, and that I should be happy instead of complaining all the time. He didn't even try to understand my feelings. I felt totally rejected.

"Well, anyway," she said as she moved her tea and leaned forward, "we came to your seminar three years ago. We had never been to a marriage seminar before. I did not know what to expect, and frankly I didn't expect much. I didn't think anybody could change Jim. During and after the seminar, Jim didn't say too much. He seemed to like it. He said that you were funny, but he didn't talk with me about any of the ideas in the seminar. I didn't expect him to, and I didn't ask him to. As I said, I had already given up by then.

"As you know," she said, "the seminar ended on Saturday afternoon. Saturday night and Sunday were pretty much as usual, but Monday afternoon, he came home from work and gave me a rose. 'Where did you get that?' I asked. 'I bought it from a street vendor,' he said. 'I thought you deserved a rose.' I started crying. 'Oh, Jim, that is so sweet of you.'

"In my mind," she said, "I knew he bought the rose from a Moonie. I had seen the young man selling roses that afternoon, but it didn't matter. The fact was, he had brought me a rose. On Tuesday he called me from the office at about one-thirty and asked me what I thought about his buying a pizza and bringing it home for dinner. He said he thought I might enjoy a break from cooking dinner. I told him I thought the idea was wonderful, and so he brought home a pizza and we had a fun time together. The children loved the pizza and thanked their father for bringing it. I actually gave him a hug and told him how much I enjoyed it.

"When he came home on Wednesday, he brought each of the children a box of Cracker Jacks, and he had a small potted plant for me. He said he knew the rose would die, and he thought I might like something that would be around for a while. I was beginning to think I was hallucinating! I couldn't believe what Jim was doing or why he was doing it. Thursday night after dinner, he handed me a card with a message about his not always being able to express his love to me but hoping that the card would communicate how much he cared. Again I cried, looked up at him, and could not resist hugging and kissing him. 'Why don't we get a baby-sitter on Saturday night and the two of us go out for dinner?' he suggested. 'That would be wonderful,' I said. On Friday afternoon, he stopped by the cookie shop and bought each of us one of our favorite cookies. Again, he kept it as a surprise, telling us only that he had a treat for dessert.

"By Saturday night," she said, "I was in orbit. I had no idea what had come over Jim, or if it would last, but I was enjoying every minute of it. After our dinner at the restaurant, I said to him, 'Jim, you have to tell me what's happening. I don't understand.'"

She looked at me intently and said, "Dr. Chapman, you have to understand. This man had never given me a flower since the day we got married. He never gave me a card for any occasion. He always said, 'It's a waste of money; you look at the card and throw it away.' We'd been out to dinner one time in five years. He never bought the children anything and expected me to buy only the essentials. He had never brought a pizza home for dinner. He expected me to have dinner ready every night. I mean, this was a radical change in his behavior."

I turned to Jim and asked, "What did you say to her in the restaurant when she asked you what was going on?"

"I told her that I had listened to your lecture on love languages at the seminar and that I realized that her love language was gifts. I also realized that I had not given her a gift in years, maybe not since we had been married. I remembered that when we were dating I used to bring her flowers and other small gifts, but after marriage I figured we couldn't afford that. I told her that I had decided that I was going to try to get her a gift every day for one week and see if it made any difference in her. I had to admit that I had seen a pretty big difference in her attitude during the week.

"I told her that I realized that what you said was really true and that learning the right love language was the key to helping another person feel loved. I said I was sorry that I had been so dense for all those years and had failed to meet her need for love. I told her that I really loved her and that I appreciated all the things she did for me and the children. I told her that with God's help, I was going to be a gift giver for the rest of my life.

"She said, 'But, Jim, you can't go on buying me gifts every day for the rest of your life. You can't afford that.' 'Well, maybe not every day,' I said, 'but at least once a week. That would be fifty-two more gifts per year than what you have received in the past five years.' I continued, 'And who said I was going to buy all of them? I might even make some of them, or I'll take Dr. Chapman's idea and pick a free flower from the front yard in the spring.'"

Janice interrupted, "Dr. Chapman, I don't think he has missed a single week in three years. He is like a new man. You wouldn't believe how happy we have been. Our children call us lovebirds now. My tank is full and overflowing."

I turned to Jim and asked, "But what about you, Jim? Do you feel loved by Janice?"

"Oh, I've always felt loved by her, Dr. Chapman. She is the best housekeeper in the world. She is an excellent cook. She keeps my clothes washed and ironed. She is wonderful about doing things for the children. I know she loves me." He smiled and said, "Now, you know what my love language is, don't you?"

I did, and I also knew why Janice had used the word *miracle*.

Gifts need not be expensive, nor must they be given weekly. But for some individuals, their worth has nothing to do with monetary value and everything to do with love.

In chapter 7, we will clarify Jim's love language.

If your spouse's love language is *Receiving Gifts:*

1. Try a parade of gifts: leave a box of candy for your spouse in the morning (yogurt candy if health is an issue); have flowers delivered in the afternoon (unless your spouse is allergic to flowers); give him a shirt in the evening. When your spouse asks, "What is going on?" you respond: "Just trying to fill your love tank!"

2. Let nature be your guide: The next time you take a walk through the neighborhood, keep your eyes open for a gift for your spouse. It may be a stone, a stick, or a flower (be sure to ask your neighbor, if the flower is not in your own yard). You may even attach special meaning to your natural gift. For example, a smooth stone may symbolize your marriage with many of the rough places now polished. A rose may remind you of the beauty you see in your spouse.

3. Discover the value of "handmade originals." Make a gift for your spouse. This may require you to enroll in an art or crafts class: ceramics, silversmithing, painting, wood carving, etc. Your main purpose for enrolling is to make your spouse a gift. A handmade gift often becomes a family heirloom.

4. Give your spouse a gift every day for one week. It need not be a special week, just any week. I promise you it will become "The Week That Was!" If you are really energetic, you can make it "The Month That Was!" No—your spouse will not expect you to keep this up for a lifetime.

5. Keep a "Gift Idea Notebook." Every time you hear your spouse say: "I really like that," or "Oh, I would really like to have one of those!" write it down in your notebook. Listen carefully and you will get quite a list. This will serve as a guide when you get ready to select a gift. To prime the pump, you may look through a shopping catalog together.

6. "Help! I'm confused!" If you really don't have a clue as to how to select a gift for your spouse, ask a friend or family member who knows your wife or husband well to help you. Most people enjoy making a friend happy by getting them a gift, especially if it is with your money.

7. Offer the gift of presence. Say to your spouse: "I want to offer the gift of my presence at any event or on any occasion you would like this month. You tell me when, and I will make every effort to be there." Get ready! Be positive! Who knows, you may enjoy the symphony or the hockey game.

8. Give your spouse a book and agree to read it yourself. Then offer to discuss together a chapter each week. Don't choose a book that you want him or her to read. Choose a book on a topic in which you know your spouse has an interest: sex, football, needlework, money management, child rearing, religion, or backpacking.

9. Give a lasting tribute. Give a substantial gift to your spouse's church or favorite charity in honor of her birthday, your anniversary, or another occasion. Ask the charity to send a card informing your spouse of what you have done. The church or charity will be excited and so will your spouse.

10. Give a living gift. Purchase and plant a tree or flowering shrub in honor of your spouse. You may plant it in your own yard, where you can water and nurture it, or in a public park or forest where others can also enjoy it. You will get credit for this one year after year. If it is an apple tree, you may live long enough to get an apple. One warning: Don't plant a crab apple tree!

THE FIVE LOVE LANGUAGES

Words of Affirmation

Quality Time

Receiving Gifts

ACTS OF SERVICE

Physical Touch

LOVE LANGUAGE #4: *Acts of Service*

Before we leave Jim and Janice, let's reexamine Jim's answer to my question, "Do you feel loved by Janice?"

"Oh, I've always felt loved by her, Dr. Chapman. She is the best housekeeper in the world. She is an excellent cook. She keeps my clothes washed and ironed. She is wonderful about doing things with the children. I know she loves me."

Jim's primary love language was what I call "acts of service." By acts of service, I mean doing things you know your spouse would like you to do. You seek to please her by serving her, to express your love for her by doing things for her.

Such actions as cooking a meal, setting a table, washing dishes, vacuuming, cleaning a commode, getting hairs out of the sink, removing the white spots from the mirror, getting bugs off the windshield, taking out the garbage, changing the baby's diaper, painting a bedroom, dusting the bookcase, keeping the car in operating condition, washing or vacuuming the car, cleaning the garage, mowing the grass, trimming the shrubs, raking the leaves, dusting the blinds, walking the dog, changing the cat's litter box, and changing water in the goldfish bowl are all acts of service. They require thought, planning, time, effort, and energy. If done with a positive spirit, they are indeed expressions of love.

A SCARLET ZINNIA: "Constancy."

Jesus Christ gave a simple but profound illustration of expressing love by an act of service when He washed the feet of His disciples. In a culture where people wore sandals and walked on dirt streets, it was customary for the servant of the household to wash the feet of guests as they arrived. Jesus, who had instructed His disciples to love one another, gave them an example of how to express that love when He took a basin and a towel and proceeded to wash their feet.[1] After that simple expression of love, He encouraged His disciples to follow His example.

Earlier in His life, Jesus had indicated that in His kingdom those who would be great would be servants. In most societies, those who are great lord it over those who are small, but Jesus Christ said that those who are great would serve others. The apostle Paul summarized that philosophy when he said, "Serve one another in love."[2]

I discovered the impact of "acts of service" in the little village of China Grove, North Carolina. China Grove sits in central North Carolina, originally nestled in chinaberry trees, not far from Andy Griffith's legendary Mayberry, and an hour and a half from Mount Pilot. At the time of this story, China Grove was a textile town with a population of 1,500. I had been away for more than ten years, studying anthropology, psychology, and theology. I was making my semiannual visit to keep in touch with my roots.

Almost everyone I knew except Dr. Shin and Dr. Smith worked in the mill. Dr. Shin was the medical doctor, and Dr. Smith was the dentist. And of course, there was Preacher Blackburn, who was pastor of the church. For most couples in China Grove, life centered on work and church. The conversation at the mill focused on the superintendent's latest decision and how it affected their job in particular. The services at church focused mainly on the anticipated joys of heaven. In that pristine American setting, I discovered love language number four.

I was standing under a chinaberry tree after church on Sunday when Mark and Mary approached me. I didn't recognize either of them. I assumed they had grown up while I was away. Introducing himself, Mark said, "I understand you have been studying counseling."

I smiled and said, "Well, a little bit."

"I have a question," he said. "Can a couple make it in marriage if they disagree on everything?"

It was one of those theoretical questions that I knew had a personal root. I brushed aside the theoretical nature of his question and asked him a personal question. "How long have you been married?"

"Two years," he responded. "And we don't agree on anything."

"Give me some examples," I continued.

"Well, for one thing, Mary doesn't like me to go hunting. I work all week in the mill, and I like to go hunting on Saturdays—not every Saturday but when hunting season is in."

Mary had been silent until this point when she interjected. "When hunting season is out, he goes fishing, and besides that, he doesn't hunt just on Saturdays. He takes off from work to go hunting."

"Once or twice a year I take off two or three days from work to go hunting in the mountains with some buddies. I don't think there is anything wrong with that."

"What else do you disagree on?" I asked.

"Well, she wants me to go to church all the time. I don't mind going on Sunday morning, but Sunday night I like to rest. It's all right if she wants to go, but I don't think I ought to have to go."

Again, Mary spoke up. "You don't really want me to go either," she said. "You fuss every time I walk out the door."

I knew that things weren't supposed to be getting this hot under a shady tree in front of a church. As a young, aspiring counselor, I feared that I was getting in over my head, but having been trained to ask questions and listen, I continued. "What other things do you disagree on?"

This time Mary answered. "He wants me to stay home all day and work in the house," she said. "He gets mad if I go see my mother or go shopping or something."

"I don't mind her going to see her mother," he said, "but when I come home, I like to see the house cleaned up. Some weeks, she doesn't make the bed up for three or four days, and half the time, she hasn't even started supper. I work hard, and I like to eat when I get home. Besides that, the house is a wreck," he continued. "The baby's things are all over the floor, the baby is dirty, and I don't like filth. She seems to be happy to live in a pigpen. We don't have very much, and we live in a small mill house, but at least it could be clean."

"What's wrong with his helping me around the house?" Mary asked. "He acts like a husband shouldn't do anything around the house. All he wants to do is work and hunt. He expects me to do everything. He even expects me to wash the car."

Thinking that I had better start looking for solutions rather than prying for more disagreements, I looked at Mark and asked, "Mark, when you were dating, before you got married, did you go hunting every Saturday?"

"Most Saturdays," he said, "but I always got home in time to go see her on Saturday night. Most of the time, I'd get home in time to wash my truck before I went to see her. I didn't like to go see her with a dirty truck."

"Mary, how old were you when you got married?" I asked.

"I was eighteen," she said. "We got married right after I finished high school. Mark graduated a year before me, and he was working."

"During your senior year in high school, how often did Mark come to see you?" I inquired.

"He came almost every night," she said. "In fact, he came in the afternoon and would often stay and have supper with my family. He would help me do my chores around the house and then we'd sit and talk until supper time."

"Mark, what did the two of you do after supper?" I asked.

Mark looked up with a sheepish smile and said, "Well, the regular dating stuff, you know."

"But if I had a school project," Mary said, "he'd help me with it. Sometimes we worked hours on school projects. I was in charge of the Christmas float for the senior class. He helped me for three weeks every afternoon. He was great."

I switched gears and focused on the third area of their disagreement. "Mark, when you were dating, did you go to church with Mary on Sunday nights?"

"Yes, I did," he said. "If I didn't go to church with her, I couldn't see her that night. Her father was strict that way."

"He never complained about it," Mary said. "In fact, he seemed to enjoy it. He even helped us with the Christmas program. After we finished the Christmas float project, we started working on the set for the Christmas program at the church. We spent about two weeks working together on that. He is really talented when it comes to painting and building sets."

I thought I was beginning to see some light, but I wasn't sure Mark and Mary were seeing it. I turned to Mary and asked, "When you were dating Mark, what convinced you that he really loved you? What made him different from other guys you had dated?"

"It was the way he helped me with everything," she said. "He was so eager to help me. None of the other guys ever expressed any interest in those things, but it seemed natural for Mark. He even helped me wash dishes when he had supper at our house. He was the most wonderful person I had ever met, but after we got married that changed. He didn't help me at all."

Turning to Mark I asked, "Why do you think you did all those things for and with her before you were married?"

"It just seemed natural for me," he said. "It's what I would want someone to do for me if she cared about me."

"And why do you think you stopped helping her after you got married?" I asked.

"Well, I guess I expected it to be like my family. Dad worked, and Mom took care of things at the house. I never saw my dad vacuum the floor or wash the dishes or do anything around the house. Since Mom didn't work outside the house, she kept everything spotless, did all the cooking, washing, and ironing. And I guess I just thought that was the way it was supposed to be."

Hoping that Mark was seeing what I was seeing, I asked, "Mark, a moment ago what did you hear Mary say when I asked her what really made her feel loved by you when you were dating?"

He responded, "Helping her with things and doing things with her."

"So, can you understand," I continued, "how she could feel unloved when you stopped helping her with things?" His head was bobbing up and down. I continued. "It was a normal thing for you to follow the model of your mother and father in marriage. Almost all of us tend to do that, but your behavior toward Mary was a radical change from your courtship. The one thing that had assured her of your love disappeared."

Then I turned to Mary and asked, "What did you hear Mark say when I asked, 'Why did you do all of those things to help Mary when you were dating?'"

"He said that it came naturally to him," she replied.

"That's right," I said, "and he also said that is what he would want someone to do for him if she loved him. He was doing those things for you and with you because in his mind that's the way anyone shows love. Once you were married and living in your own house, he had expectations of what you would do if you loved him. You would keep the house clean, you would cook, and so on. In brief, you would do things for him to express your love. When he did not see you doing those things, do you understand why he would feel unloved?" Mary's head was also bobbing now. I continued, "My guess is that the reason you are both so unhappy in your marriage is that neither of you is showing your love by doing things for each other."

Mary said, "I think you are right, and the reason I stopped doing things for him is because I resented his demanding spirit. It was as if he were trying to make me be like his mother."

"You are right," I said, "and no one likes to be forced to do anything. In fact, love is always freely given. Love cannot be demanded. We can request things of each other, but we must never demand anything. Requests give direction to love, but demands stop the flow of love."

Mark broke in and said, "She's right, Dr. Chapman. I was demanding and critical of her because I was disappointed in her as a wife. I know I said some cruel things, and I understand how she could be upset with me."

"I think things can be turned around rather easily at this juncture," I said. I pulled two note cards out of my pocket. "Let's try something. I want each of you to sit on the steps of the church and make a request list. Mark, I want you to list three or four things that if Mary chose to do them would make you feel loved when you walk into the house in the afternoon. If making the bed is important to you, then put it down. Mary, I want you to make a list of three or four things that you would really like to have Mark's help in doing, things which, if he chose to do them, would help you know that he loved you." (I'm big on lists; they force us to think concretely.)

After five to six minutes, they handed me their lists. Mark's list read:

- Make up the beds every day.

- Have the baby's face washed when I get home.

- Put her shoes in the closet before I get home.

- Try to have supper at least started before I get home so that we could eat within 30–45 minutes after I get home.

Requests give direction to love, but demands stop the flow of love.

I read the list out loud and said to Mark, "I'm understanding you to say that if Mary chooses to do these four things, you will view them as acts of love toward you."

"That's right," he said, "if she did those four things, it would go a long way in changing my attitude toward her." Then I read Mary's list:

- I wish he would wash the car every week instead of expecting me to do it.

- I wish he would change the baby's diaper after he gets home in the afternoon, especially if I am working on supper.

- I wish he would vacuum the house for me once a week.

- I wish he would mow the grass every week in the summer and not let it get so tall that I am ashamed of our yard.

I said, "Mary, I am understanding you to say that if Mark chooses to do those four things, you would take his actions as genuine expressions of love toward you."

"That's right," she said. "It would be wonderful if he would do those things for me."

"Does this list seem reasonable to you, Mark? Is it feasible for you to do these things?"

"Yes," he said.

"Mary, do the things on Mark's list seem reasonable and feasible to you? Could you do them if you chose to?"

"Yes," she said, "I can do those things. In the past, I have felt overwhelmed because no matter what I did, it was never enough."

"Mark," I said, "you understand that what I am suggesting is a change from the model of marriage that your mother and father had."

"Oh," he said, "my father mowed the grass and washed the car."

"But he didn't change the diapers or vacuum the floor, right?"

"Right," he said.

"You don't have to do these, you understand? If you do them, however, it will be an act of love to Mary."

And to Mary I said, "You understand that you don't have to do these things, but if you want to express love for Mark, here are four ways that will be meaningful to him. I want to suggest that you try these for two months and see if they help. At the end of two months, you may want to add additional requests to your lists and share them with each other. I would not add more than one request per month, however."

"This really makes sense," Mary said. "I think you have helped us," Mark said. They took each other by the hand and walked toward their car. I said to myself out loud, "I think this is what church is all about. I think I am going to enjoy being a counselor." I have never forgotten the insight I gained under that chinaberry tree.

After years of research, I have realized what a unique situation Mark and Mary presented me. Seldom do I meet a couple who both have the same love language. For both Mark and Mary, "acts of service" was their primary love language. Hundreds of individuals can identify with either Mark or Mary and acknowledge that the primary way that they feel loved is by acts of service on the part of their spouse. Putting away shoes, changing a baby's diaper, washing dishes or a car, vacuuming, or mowing speaks volumes to the individual whose primary love language is acts of service.

What we do for each other before marriage is no indication of what we will do after marriage.

You may be wondering, *If Mark and Mary had the same primary love language, why were they having so much difficulty?* The answer lies in the fact that they were speaking different dialects. They were doing things for each other but not the most important things. When they were forced to think concretely, they easily identified their specific dialects. For Mary it was washing the car, changing the baby's diaper, vacuuming the floor, and mowing the grass, whereas for Mark it was making up the bed, washing the baby's face, putting the shoes in the closet, and having supper underway when he got home from work. When they started speaking the right dialects, their love tanks began to fill. Since acts of service was their primary love language, learning each other's specific dialect was relatively easy for them.

Before we leave Mark and Mary, I would like to make three other observations. First, they illustrate clearly that what we do for each other before marriage is no indication of what we will do after marriage. Before marriage, we are carried along by the force of the in-love obsession. After marriage, we revert to being the people we were before we "fell in love." Our actions are influenced by the model of our parents, our own personality, our perceptions of love, our emotions, needs, and desires. Only one thing is certain about our behavior: It will not be the same behavior we exhibited when we were caught up in being "in love."

That leads me to the second truth illustrated by Mark and Mary. Love is a choice and cannot be coerced. Mark and Mary were criticizing each other's behavior and getting nowhere. Once they decided to make requests of each other rather than demands, their marriage began to turn around. Criticism and demands tend to drive wedges. With enough criticism, you may get acquiescence from your spouse. He may do what you want, but probably it will not be an expression of love. You can give guidance to love by making requests: "I wish you would wash the car, change the baby's diaper, mow the grass," but you cannot create the will to love. Each of us must decide daily to love or not to love our spouses. If we choose to love, then expressing it in the way in which our spouse requests will make our love most effective emotionally.

There is a third truth, which only the mature lover will be able to hear. My spouse's criticisms about my behavior provide me with the clearest clue to her primary love language. People tend to criticize their spouse most loudly in the area where they themselves have the deepest emotional need. Their criticism is an ineffective way of pleading for love. If we understand that, it may help us process their criticism in a more productive manner. A wife may say to her husband after he gives her a criticism, "It sounds like that is extremely important to you. Could you explain why it is so crucial?" Criticism often needs clarification. Initiating such a conversation may eventually turn the criticism into a request rather than a demand. Mary's constant condemnation of Mark's hunting was not an expression of her hatred for the sport of hunting. She blamed hunting as the thing that kept him from washing the car, vacuuming the house, and mowing the grass. When he learned to meet her need for love by speaking her emotional love language, she became free to support him in his hunting.

Doormat or Lover?

"I have served him for twenty years. I have waited on him hand and foot. I have been his doormat while he ignored me, mistreated me, and humiliated me in front my friends and family. I don't hate him. I wish him no ill, but I resent him, and I no longer wish to live with him." That wife has performed acts of service for twenty years, but they have not been expressions of love. They were done out of fear, guilt, and resentment.

A doormat is an inanimate object. You can wipe your feet on it, step on it, kick it around, or whatever you like. It has no will of its own. It can be your servant but not your lover. When we treat our spouses as objects, we preclude the possibility of love. Manipulation by guilt ("If you were a good spouse, you would do this for me") is not the language of love. Coercion by fear ("You will

Due to the sociological changes of the past thirty years, there is no longer a common stereotype of the male and female role in American society.

do this or you will be sorry") is alien to love. No person should ever be a doormat. We may allow ourselves to be used, but we are in fact creatures of emotion, thoughts, and desires. And we have the ability to make decisions and take action. Allowing oneself to be used or manipulated by another is not an act of love. It is, in fact, an action of treason. You are allowing him or her to develop inhumane habits. Love says, "I love you too much to let you treat me this way. It is not good for you or me."

Overcoming Stereotypes

Learning the love language of acts of service will require some of us to reexamine our stereotypes of the roles of husbands and wives. Mark was doing what most of us do naturally. He was following the role model of his father and mother, but he wasn't even doing that well. His father washed the car and mowed the grass. Mark did not, but that was the mental image he had of what a husband should do. He definitely did not picture himself vacuuming floors and changing the baby's diapers. To his credit, he was willing to break from his stereotype when he realized how important it was to Mary. That is necessary for all of us if our spouse's primary love language asks something of us that seems inappropriate to our role.

Due to the sociological changes of the past thirty years, there is no longer a common stereotype of the male and female role in American society. Yet that does not mean that all stereotypes have been removed. It means rather that the number of stereotypes has been multiplied. Before the days of television, a person's idea of what a husband or wife should do and how he or she should relate was influenced primarily by one's own parents. With the pervasiveness of television and the proliferation of single-parent families, however, role models are often influenced by forces outside the home. Whatever your perceptions, chances are your spouse perceives marital roles somewhat differently than you do. A willingness to examine and change stereotypes is necessary in order to express love more effectively. Remember, there are no rewards for maintaining stereotypes, but there are tremendous benefits to meeting the emotional needs of your spouse.

Recently a wife said to me, "Dr. Chapman, I am going to send all of my friends to your seminar."

"And why would you do that?" I inquired.

"Because it has radically changed our marriage," she said. "Before the seminar, Bob never helped me with anything. We both started our careers right after college, but it was always my role to do everything at the house. It was as if it never crossed his mind to help me with anything. After the seminar, he started asking me, 'What can I do to help you this evening?' It was amazing. At first, I couldn't believe it was real, but it has persisted for three years now.

"I'll have to admit, there were some trying and humorous times in those early weeks because he didn't know how to do anything. The first time he did the laundry, he used undiluted bleach instead of regular detergent. Our blue towels came out with white polka dots. Then there was the first time he used the garbage disposal. It sounded strange, and shortly afterward soap bubbles started emerging from the drain of the adjoining sink. He didn't know what was happening until I turned the garbage disposal off, reached my hand inside, and retrieved the remains of a new bar of soap, now the size of a quarter. But he was loving me in my language, and my tank was filling up. Now he knows how to do everything around the house and is always helping me. We have much more time together because I don't have to work all the time. Believe me, I have learned his language, and I keep his tank full."

Is it really that simple?

Simple? Yes. Easy? No. Bob had to work hard at tearing down the stereotype with which he had lived for thirty-five years. It didn't come easily, but he would tell you that learning the primary love language of your spouse and choosing to speak it makes a tremendous difference in the emotional climate of a marriage. Now, let's move on to love language number five.

NOTES
1. John 13:3–17.
2. Galatians 5:13.

If your spouse's love language is *Acts of Service:*

1. Make a list of all the requests your spouse has made of you over the past few weeks. Select one of these each week and do it as an expression of love.

2. Cut out some heart-shaped note cards and print the following:

   "Today I will show my love for you by . . ." Complete the sentence with one of the following: mowing the lawn, vacuuming the floor, washing dishes, taking the dog for a walk, cleaning the fish bowl, etc.

   Give your spouse a love note accompanied by the act of service every three days for a month.

3. Ask your spouse to make a list of ten things he or she would like for you to do during the next month. Then ask your spouse to prioritize those by numbering them 1–10, with 1 being the most important and 10 being least important. Use this list to plan your strategy for a month of love. (Get ready to live with a happy spouse.)

4. While your spouse is away, get the children to help you with some act of service for him. When he walks in the door, join the children in shouting "Surprise! We love you!" Then share your act of service.

5. What one act of service has your spouse nagged about consistently? Why not decide to see the nag as a tag? Your spouse is tagging this as really important to him or her. If you choose to do it as an expression of love, it is worth more than a thousand roses.

6. If your spouse's requests for acts of service come across as nags or put-downs, try writing them in words that would be less offensive to you. Share this revised wording with your spouse. For example, "Honey, I love you so much. You are a hardworking man and I really appreciate you. I'd love to thank you in advance for mowing the lawn this week before Thursday when Mary and Bob come over for dinner." Your husband might even respond: "Where is the lawn mower, I can't wait!" Try it and see.

7. Do some major acts of service like washing the car, cooking a meal, painting a bedroom, or washing the deck, and then post a sign that reads, "To (spouse's name) with love," and sign your name.

8. If you have more money than time, hire someone to do the acts of service that you know your spouse would like for you to do, such as the lawn, the housecleaning, the car washing, the laundry. If you take the responsibility for getting it done, you will be speaking love even when you are away.

9. Ask your spouse to tell you the daily acts of service that would really speak love to him or her. These might include such things as putting your dirty clothes in the hamper, getting the hairs out of the sink, hanging up your clothes at night, closing the door when you go outside, preparing a meal, and washing the dishes. Seek to work these into your daily schedule. "Little things" really do mean a lot.

10. Periodically ask your spouse, "If I could do one special act of service this week, what would you request?" If possible, do it and watch your spouse's love tank fill up!

THE FIVE LOVE LANGUAGES

Words of Affirmation

Quality Time

Receiving Gifts

Acts of Service

PHYSICAL TOUCH

LOVE LANGUAGE #5: *Physical Touch*

We have long known that physical touch is a way of communicating emotional love. Numerous research projects in the area of child development have made that conclusion: Babies who are held, hugged, and kissed develop a healthier emotional life than those who are left for long periods of time without physical contact. The importance of touching children is not a modern idea. In the first century, the Hebrews living in Palestine, recognizing Jesus as a great teacher, brought their children to Him "to have him touch them."[1] You may remember that Jesus' disciples rebuked those parents, thinking that Jesus was too busy for such frivolous activity. But the Scriptures say that Jesus was indignant with the disciples and said, "'Let the little children come to me, and do not hinder them, for the kingdom of God belongs to such as these. I tell you the truth, anyone who will not receive the kingdom of God like a little child will never enter it.' And he took the children in his arms, put his hands on them and blessed them."[2] Wise parents, in any culture, are touching parents.

A SINGLE RED ROSE: *"I love you."*

Physical touch is also a powerful vehicle for communicating marital love. Holding hands, kissing, embracing, and sexual intercourse are all ways of communicating emotional love to one's spouse. For some individuals, physical touch is their primary love language. Without it, they feel unloved. With it, their emotional tank is filled, and they feel secure in the love of their spouse.

The old-timers used to say, "The way to a man's heart is through his stomach." Many a man has been "fattened for the kill" by women who have believed this philosophy. The old-timers, of course, were not thinking of the physical heart but of man's romantic center. It would be more accurate to say, "The way to some men's hearts is through their stomachs." I remember the husband who said, "Dr. Chapman, my wife is a gourmet cook. She spends hours in the kitchen. She makes these elaborate meals. Me? I'm a meat and potatoes man. I tell her she is wasting her time. I like simple food. She gets hurt and says I don't appreciate her. I do appreciate her. I just wish she would make it easy on herself and not spend so much time with the elaborate meals. Then we would have more time together, and she would have the energy to do some other things." Obviously, "other things" were closer to his heart than fancy foods.

That man's wife was a frustrated lover. In the family in which she grew up, her mother was an excellent cook and her father appreciated her efforts. She remembers hearing her father say to her mother, "When I sit down to meals like this, it's so easy for me to love you." Her father was a wellspring of positive comments to her mother about her cooking. In private and in public, he praised her culinary skills. That daughter learned well from her mother's model. The problem is that she is not married to her father. Her husband has a different love language.

In my conversation with this husband, it didn't take long to discover that "other things" to him meant sex. When his wife was sexually responsive, he felt secure in her love. But when, for whatever reason, she withdrew from him sexually, all of her culinary skills could not convince him that she really loved him. He did not object to the fancy meals, but in his heart they could never substitute for what he considered to be "love."

Sexual intercourse, however, is only one dialect in the love language of physical touch. Of the five senses, touching, unlike the other four, is not limited to one localized area of the body. Tiny, tactile receptors are located throughout the body. When those receptors are touched or pressed, nerves carry impulses to the brain. The brain interprets these impulses and we perceive that the thing that touched us is warm or cold, hard or soft. It causes pain or pleasure. We may also interpret it as loving or hostile.

Some parts of the body are more sensitive than others. The difference is due to the fact that the tiny tactile receptors are not scattered evenly over the body but arranged in clusters. Thus, the tip of the tongue is highly sensitive to touch whereas the back of the shoulders is the least sensitive. The tips of the fingers and the tip of the nose are other extremely sensitive areas. Our purpose, however, is not to understand the neurological basis of the sense of touch but rather its psychological importance.

Physical touch can make or break a relationship. It can communicate hate or love. To the person whose primary love language is physical touch, the message will be far louder than the words "I hate you" or "I love you." A slap in the face is detrimental to any child, but it is devastating to a child whose primary love language is touch. A tender hug communicates love to any child, but it shouts love to the child whose primary love language is physical touch. The same is true of adults.

Physical touch can make or break a relationship. It can communicate hate or love.

In marriage, the touch of love may take many forms. Since touch receptors are located throughout the body, lovingly touching your spouse almost anywhere can be an expression of love. That does not mean that all touches are created equal. Some will bring more pleasure to your spouse than others. Your best instructor is your spouse, of course. After all, she is the one you are seeking to love. She knows best what she perceives as a loving touch. Don't insist on touching her in your way and in your time. Learn to speak her love dialect. Your spouse may find some touches uncomfortable or irritating. To insist on continuing those touches is to communicate the opposite of love. It is saying that you are not sensitive to her needs and that you care little about her perceptions of what is pleasant. Don't make the mistake of believing that the touch that brings pleasure to you will also bring pleasure to her.

Love touches may be explicit and demand your full attention such as in a back rub or sexual foreplay, culminating in intercourse. On the other hand, love touches may be implicit and require only a moment, such as putting your hand on his shoulder as you pour a cup of coffee or rubbing your body against him as you pass in the kitchen. Explicit love touches obviously take more time, not only in actual touching but in developing your understanding of how to communicate love to your spouse this way. If a back massage communicates love loudly to your spouse, then the time, money, and energy you spend in learning to be a good masseur or masseuse will be well invested. If sexual intercourse is your mate's primary dialect, reading about and discussing the art of sexual lovemaking will enhance your expression of love.

Implicit love touches require little time but much thought, especially if physical touch is not your primary love language and if you did not grow up in a "touching family." Sitting close to each other on the couch as you watch your favorite television program requires no additional time but may communicate your love loudly. Touching your spouse as you walk through the room where he is sitting takes only a moment. Touching each other when you leave the house and again when you return may involve only a brief kiss or hug but will speak volumes to your spouse.

Once you discover that physical touch is the primary love language of your spouse, you are limited only by your imagination on ways to express love. Coming up with new ways and places to touch can be an exciting challenge. If you have not been an "under-the-table toucher," you might find that it will add a spark to your dining out. If you are not accustomed to holding hands in public, you may find that you can fill your spouse's emotional love tank as you stroll through the parking lot. If you don't normally kiss as soon as you get into the car together, you may find that it will greatly enhance your travels. Hugging your spouse before she goes shopping may not only express love, it may bring her home sooner. Try new touches in new places and let your spouse give you feedback on whether he finds it pleasurable or not. Remember, he has the final word. You are learning to speak his language.

The Body Is for Touching

Whatever there is of me resides in my body. To touch my body is to touch me. To withdraw from my body is to distance yourself from me emotionally. In our society shaking hands is a way of communicating openness and social closeness to another individual. When, on rare occasions one man refuses to shake hands with another, it communicates a message that things are not right in their relationship. All societies have some form of physical touching as a means of social greeting. The average American male may not feel comfortable with the European bear hug and kiss, but in Europe that serves the same function as our shaking hands.

If your spouse's primary love language is physical touch, nothing is more important than holding her as she cries.

There are appropriate and inappropriate ways to touch members of the opposite sex in every society. The recent attention to sexual harassment has highlighted the inappropriate ways. Within marriage, however, what is appropriate and inappropriate touching is determined by the couple themselves, within certain broad guidelines. Physical abuse is of course deemed inappropriate by society, and social organizations have been formed to help "the battered wife and the battered husband." Clearly our bodies are for touching, but not for abuse.

This age is characterized as the age of sexual openness and freedom. With that freedom, we have demonstrated that the open marriage where both spouses are free to have sexual intimacies with other individuals is fanciful. Those who do not object on moral grounds eventually object on emotional grounds. Something about our need for intimacy and love does not allow us to give our spouse such freedom. The emotional pain is deep and intimacy evaporates when we are aware that our spouse is involved with someone else sexually. Counselors' files are filled with records of husbands and wives who are trying to grapple with the emotional trauma of an unfaithful spouse. That trauma, however, is compounded for the individual whose primary love language is physical touch. That for which he longs so deeply—love expressed by physical touch—is now being given to another. His emotional love tank is not only empty; it has been riddled by an explosion. It will take massive repairs for those emotional needs to be met.

Crisis and Physical Touch

Almost instinctively in a time of crisis, we hug one another. Why? Because physical touch is a powerful communicator of love. In a time of crisis, more than anything, we need to feel loved. We cannot always change events, but we can survive if we feel loved.

All marriages will experience crises. The death of parents is inevitable. Automobile accidents cripple and kill thousands each year. Disease is no respecter of persons. Disappointments are a part of life. The most important thing you can do for your mate in a time of crisis is to love him or her. If your spouse's primary love language is physical touch, nothing is more important than holding her as she cries. Your words may mean little, but your physical touch will communicate that you care. Crises provide a unique opportunity for expressing love. Your tender touches will be remembered long after the crisis has passed. Your failure to touch may never be forgotten.

Since my first visit to West Palm Beach, Florida, many years ago, I have always welcomed invitations to lead marriage seminars in that area. It was on one such occasion that I met Pete and Patsy. They were not native to Florida (few are), but they had lived there for twenty years and called West Palm Beach home. My seminar was sponsored by a local church, and as we drove from the airport, the pastor informed me that Pete and Patsy had requested that I spend the night at their house. I tried to act excited, but knew from experience that such a request usually meant a late-night counseling session. However, I was to be surprised in more than one way that night.

As the pastor and I entered the spacious, well-decorated, Spanish-style house, I was introduced to Patsy and to Charlie, the family cat. As I looked around the house, I had the hunch that either Pete's business had done very well, his father had left him a huge inheritance, or he was hopelessly in debt. Later I discovered that my first hunch was correct. When I was shown the guest room, I observed that Charlie, the cat, was making himself at home, stretched across the bed where I was to be sleeping. I thought, *This cat has it made.*

Pete came home shortly, and we had a delightful snack together and agreed that we would have dinner after the seminar. Several hours later while sharing dinner, I kept waiting for the counseling session to begin. It never did. Instead, I found Pete and Patsy to be a healthy, happily married couple. For a counselor, that is an oddity. I was eager to discover their secret, but being extremely tired and knowing that Pete and Patsy were going to drive me to the airport the next day, I decided to do my probing when I was feeling more alert. They showed me to my room.

Charlie, the cat, was nice enough to leave the room when I got there. Bounding from the bed, he headed off to another bedroom and within minutes, I was in bed. After a brief reflection of the day, I was entering the twilight zone. Just before losing touch with reality, the door to my bedroom popped open and a monster leaped on top of me! I had heard of Florida's scorpions, but this was no small scorpion. Without time to think, I grabbed the sheet that was draped over my body and with one bloodcurdling shriek, flung the monster against the far wall. I heard his body hit the wall and then silence. Pete and Patsy came running down the hallway, turned on the light, and we all looked at Charlie lying still.

Pete and Patsy have never forgotten me, and I have never forgotten them. Charlie did revive in a few minutes, but he did not come back to my room. In fact, Pete and Patsy told me later that Charlie never went back to that bedroom again.

After my abuse of Charlie, I wasn't sure whether Pete and Patsy would still want to take me to the airport the next day or if they would have any further interest in me. However, my fears vanished when, after the seminar, Pete said, "Dr. Chapman, I have been to many seminars, but I have never heard anyone describe Patsy and me as clearly as you. That love language idea is true. I can't wait to tell you our story!"

A few minutes after saying good-byes to those attending the seminar, we were in the car for our forty-five-minute drive to the airport. And Pete and Patsy began to tell me their story. In the early years of their marriage, they had tremendous difficulties. but some twenty-two years earlier, all of their friends agreed that they were the "perfect couple." Pete and Patsy certainly believed that their marriage was "made in heaven."

They had grown up in the same community, attended the same church, and graduated from the same high school. Their parents had similar lifestyles and values. Pete and Patsy enjoyed many of the same things. They both liked tennis and boating, and they often talked about how many interests they held in common. They seemed to possess all the commonalities that are supposed to assure fewer conflicts in marriage.

They began dating in their senior year in high school. They attended separate colleges but managed to see each other at least once a month and sometimes more often. By the end of their freshman year, they were convinced that they were "meant for each other." They both agreed, however, to finish college before marriage. For the next three years, they enjoyed an idyllic dating relationship. One weekend, he would visit her campus; the following weekend, she would visit his campus; the third weekend, they would go home to visit the folks but spend most of the weekend with each other. The fourth weekend of each month, they agreed not to see each other, thus giving each of them freedom to develop individual interests. Except for special events such as birthdays, they consistently followed that schedule. Three weeks after he received his degree in business and she a degree in sociology, they were married. Two months later, they moved to Florida where Pete had been offered a good job. They were two thousand miles from their nearest relative. They could enjoy a "honeymoon" forever.

The first three months were exciting—moving, finding a new apartment, enjoying life together. The only conflict they could remember was over washing dishes. Pete thought he had a more efficient way to complete that chore. Patsy, however, was not open to his idea. Eventually, they had agreed that whoever washed the dishes

At the end of the first year, Patsy was desperate.

could do it his/her way, and that conflict was resolved. They were about six months into the marriage when Patsy began to feel that Pete was withdrawing from her. He was working longer hours, and when he was at home, he spent considerable time with the computer. When she finally expressed her feelings that he was avoiding her, Pete told her that he was not avoiding her but simply trying to stay on top of his job. He said that she didn't understand the pressure he was under and how important it was that he do well in his first year on the job. Patsy wasn't pleased, but she decided to give him space.

Patsy began to develop friendships with other wives who lived in the apartment complex. Often when she knew Pete was going to work late she would go shopping with one of her friends instead of going straight home after work. Sometimes she was not at home when Pete arrived. That annoyed him greatly, and he accused her of being thoughtless and irresponsible. Patsy retorted, "This is the pot calling the kettle black. Who is irresponsible? You don't even call me and let me know when you will be home. How can I be here for you when I don't even know when you will be here? And when you are here, you spend all your time with that dumb computer. You don't need a wife; all you need is a computer!"

To which Pete loudly responded, "I do need a wife. Don't you understand? That's the whole point. I do need a wife."

But Patsy did not understand. She was extremely confused. In her search for answers, she went to the public library and checked out several books on marriage. "Marriage is not supposed to be this way," she reasoned. "I have to find an answer to our situation." When Pete went to the computer room, Patsy would pick up her book. In fact on many evenings, she read until midnight. On his way to bed, Pete would notice her and make sarcastic comments such as, "If you read that much in college, you would have made straight A's." Patsy would respond, "I am not in college. I'm in marriage, and right now, I'd be satisfied with a C." Pete went to bed without so much as a second glance.

At the end of the first year, Patsy was desperate. She had mentioned it before, but this time she calmly said to Pete, "I am going to find a marriage counselor. Do you want to go with me?"

But Pete answered, "I don't need a marriage counselor. I don't have time to go to a marriage counselor. I can't afford a marriage counselor."

"Then I'll go alone," said Patsy.

"Fine, you are the one who needs counseling anyway."

The conversation was over. Patsy felt totally alone, but the next week she made an appointment with a marriage counselor. After three sessions, the counselor called Pete and asked if he would be willing to come in to talk about his perspective on their marriage. Pete agreed, and the process of healing began. Six months later, they left the counselor's office with a new marriage.

I said to Pete and Patsy, "What did you learn in counseling that turned your marriage around?"

"In essence, Dr. Chapman," Pete said, "we learned to speak each other's love language. The counselor did not use that term, but as you gave the lecture today, the lights came on. My mind raced back to our counseling experience, and I realized that's exactly what happened to us. We finally learned to speak each other's love language."

"So what is your love language, Pete?" I asked.

"Physical touch," he said without hesitation.

"Physical touch for sure," said Patsy.

"And yours, Patsy?"

"Quality time, Dr. Chapman. That's what I was crying for in those days while he was spending all his time with his job and his computer."

"How did you learn that physical touch was Pete's love language?"

"It took a while," Patsy said. "Little by little, it began to come out in the counseling. At first, I don't think Pete even realized it."

"She's right," Pete said. "I was so insecure in my own sense of self-worth that it took forever for me to be willing to identify and acknowledge that her lack of touch had caused me to withdraw. I never told her that I wanted to be touched, although I was crying inside for her to reach out and touch me. In our dating relationship, I had always taken the initiative in hugging, kissing, and holding hands, but she had always been responsive. I felt that she loved me, but after we got married, there were times that I reached out to her physically and she was not responsive. Maybe with her new job responsibilities she was too tired. I don't know, but I took it personally. I felt that she didn't find me attractive. Then I decided I would not take the initiative because I didn't want to be rejected. So I waited to see how long it would be before she'd initiate a kiss or a touch or sexual intercourse. Once I waited for six weeks before she touched me at all. I found it unbearable. My withdrawal was to stay away from the pain I felt when I was with her. I felt rejected, unwanted, and unloved."

Then Patsy said, "I had no idea that that was what he was feeling. I knew that he was not reaching out to me. We were not kissing and hugging as we had done earlier, but I just assumed that since we were married, that was not as important to him now. I knew that he was under pressure with his job. I had no idea that he wanted me to take the initiative.

"He's right. I would go weeks without touching him. It didn't cross my mind. I was preparing meals, keeping the house clean, doing his laundry, and trying to stay out of his way. I honestly didn't know what else I could be doing. I could not understand his withdrawal or his lack of attention to me. It's not that I dislike touching; it's just that it was never that important to me. Spending time with me is what made me feel loved and appreciated, giving me attention. It really didn't matter whether we hugged or kissed. As long as he gave me his attention, I felt loved.

"It took us a long time to discover the root of the problem, but once we discovered that we were not meeting each other's emotional need for love, we began to turn things around. Once I began to take the initiative in giving him physical touch, it's amazing what happened. His personality, his spirit changed drastically. I had a new husband. Once he became convinced that I really did love him, then he began to become more responsive to my needs."

"Does he still have a computer at home?" I asked.

"Yes," she said, "but he seldom uses it and when he does, it's all right because I know that he is not 'married' to the computer. We do so many things together that it's easy for me to give him the freedom to use the computer when he wants to."

"What amazed me at the seminar today," Pete said, "was the way your lecture on love languages carried me back all these years to that experience. You said in twenty minutes what it took us six months to learn."

"Well," I said, "it's not how fast you learn it but how well you learn it that matters. And obviously, you have learned it well."

Pete is only one of many individuals for whom physical touch is the primary love language. Emotionally, they yearn for their spouse to reach out and touch them physically. Running the hand through the hair, giving a back rub, holding hands, embracing, sexual intercourse—all of those and other "love touches" are the emotional lifeline of the person for whom physical touch is the primary love language.

NOTES
1. Mark 10:13.
2. Mark 10:14–16.

If your spouse's love language is *Physical Touch:*

1. As you walk from the car to the shopping mall, reach out and hold your spouse's hand. (Unless, of course, you have three preschool children with you.)

2. While eating together, let your knee or foot drift over and touch your spouse. Be careful you are not rubbing the dog.

3. Walk up to your spouse and say, "Have I told you lately that I love you?" Take her in your arms and hug her while you rub her back and continue. "You are the greatest!" (Resist the temptation to rush to the bedroom.) Untangle yourself and move on to the next thing.

4. While your spouse is seated, walk up behind her and initiate a shoulder massage. Continue for five minutes unless your spouse begs you to stop.

5. If you sit together in church, when the minister calls for prayer reach over and hold your spouse's hand.

6. Initiate sex by giving your spouse a foot massage. Continue to other parts of the body as long as it brings pleasure to your spouse.

7. Run the water in the Jacuzzi and announce to your spouse that you are looking for a partner to join you.

8. Riding down the road together, reach over and touch your spouse on the leg, stomach, arm, hand, or . . . If he or she says "stop!" by all means put on the brakes.

9. When family or friends are visiting, touch your spouse in their presence. A hug, running your hand along his or her arm, putting your arm around his as you stand talking or simply placing your hand on her shoulder can earn double emotional points. It says, "Even with all these people in our house, I still see you."

---

10. When your spouse arrives at home, meet him or her one step earlier than usual and give your mate a big hug. If you normally meet at the door, go to the garage. If you normally meet in the garage, go to the street. Then, as the car turns into the driveway, stop your mate, lean into the lowered window, and give him or her a kiss. If you normally meet at the street, hide in the parking area and step out as your mate opens the door and give him or her a hug. (Be sure your mate sees you before you hug him or her.)

THE FIVE LOVE LANGUAGES

Discovering Your
Primary Love Language

DISCOVERING YOUR PRIMARY LOVE LANGUAGE

Discovering the primary love language of your spouse is essential if you are to keep his/her emotional love tank full. But first, let's make sure you know your own love language. Having heard the five emotional love languages,

> *Words of Affirmation*
> *Quality Time*
> *Receiving Gifts*
> *Acts of Service*
> *Physical Touch*

A RED POPPY:
"Imagination, pleasure."

some individuals will know instantaneously their own primary love language and that of their spouse. For others, it will not be that easy. Some are like Bob from Parma Heights, Ohio, who after hearing the five emotional love languages said to me, "I don't know. It seems that two of those are just about equal for me."

"Which two?" I inquired.

"'Physical Touch' and 'Words of Affirmation,'" Bob responded.

"By 'Physical Touch,' what do you mean?"

"Well, mainly sex," Bob replied.

I probed a little further, asking, "Do you enjoy your wife running her hands through your hair, or giving you a back rub, or holding hands, or kissing and hugging you at times when you are not having sexual intercourse?"

"Those things are fine," said Bob. "I am not going to turn them down, but the main thing is sexual intercourse. That's when I know that she really loves me."

Leaving the subject of physical touch for a moment, I turned to affirming words and asked, "When you say that 'Words of Affirmation' are also important, what kinds of statements do you find most helpful?"

"Almost anything if it is positive," Bob replied. "When she tells me how good I look, how smart I am, what a hard worker I am, when she expresses appreciation for the things I do around the house, when she makes positive comments about my taking time with the children, when she tells me she loves me—all of those things really mean a lot to me."

"Did you receive those kinds of comments from your parents when you were growing up?"

"Not very often," Bob said. "Most of what I got from my parents were critical or demanding words. I guess that's why I appreciated Carol so much in the first place, because she gave me words of affirmation."

"Let me ask you this. If Carol were meeting your sexual needs, that is, if you were having quality sexual intercourse as often as you desire, but she was giving you negative words, making critical remarks, sometimes putting you down in front of others, do you think you would feel loved by her?"

"I don't think so," he replied. "I think I would feel betrayed and deeply hurt. I think I would be depressed."

"Bob," I said, "I think we have just discovered that your primary love language is 'Words of Affirmation.' Sexual intercourse is extremely important to you and to your sense of intimacy with Carol, but her words of affirmation are more important to you emotionally. If she were, in fact, verbally critical of you all the time and put you down in front of other people, the time may come when you would no longer desire to have sexual intercourse with her because she would be a source of deep pain to you."

Bob had made the mistake common to many men: assuming that "Physical Touch" is their primary love language because they desire sexual intercourse so intensely. For the male, sexual desire is physically based. That is, the desire for sexual intercourse is stimulated by the buildup of sperm cells and seminal fluid in the seminal vesicles. When the seminal vesicles are full, there is a physical push for release. Thus, the male's desire for sexual intercourse has a physical root.

For the female, sexual desire is rooted in her emotions, not her physiology. There is nothing physically that builds up and pushes her to have intercourse. Her desire is emotionally based. If she feels loved and admired and appreciated by her husband, then she has a desire to be physically intimate with him. But without the emotional closeness she may have little physical desire.

Because the male is physically pushed to have sexual release on a somewhat regular basis, he may automatically assume that that is his primary love language. But if he does not enjoy physical touch at other times and in nonsexual ways, it may not be his love language at all. Sexual desire is quite different from his emotional need to feel loved. That doesn't mean that sexual intercourse is unimportant to him—it is extremely important—but sexual intercourse alone will not meet his need to feel loved. His wife must speak his primary emotional love language as well.

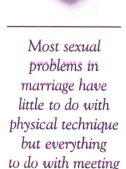

Most sexual problems in marriage have little to do with physical technique but everything to do with meeting emotional needs.

When, in fact, his wife speaks his primary love language and his emotional love tank is full, and he speaks her primary love language and her emotional tank is full, the sexual aspect of their relationship will take care of itself. Most sexual problems in marriage have little to do with physical technique but everything to do with meeting emotional needs.

After further conversation and reflection, Bob said, "You know, I think you are right. 'Words of Affirmation' is definitely my primary love language. When she has been cutting and critical of me verbally, I tend to withdraw from her sexually and fantasize about other women. But when she tells me how much she appreciates me and admires me, my natural sexual desires are turned toward her." Bob had made a significant discovery in our brief conversation.

What is your primary love language? What makes you feel most loved by your spouse? What do you desire above all else? If the answer to those questions does not leap to your mind immediately, perhaps it will help to look at the negative use of love languages. What does your spouse do or say or fail to do or say that hurts you deeply? If, for example, your deepest pain is the critical, judgmental words of your spouse, then perhaps your love language is "Words of Affirmation." If your primary love language is used negatively by your spouse—that is, he does the opposite—it will hurt you more deeply than it would hurt someone else because not only is he neglecting to speak your primary love language, he is actually using that language as a knife to your heart.

I remember Mary in Kitchener, Ontario, who said, "Dr. Chapman, what hurts me most is that Ron never lifts a hand to help me around the house. He watches television while I do all the work. I don't understand how he could do that if he really loved me." Mary's deepest hurt, mainly that Ron did not help her do things around the house, was the clue to her primary love language—"Acts of Service." If it grieves you deeply that your spouse seldom gives you a gift for any occasion, then perhaps your primary love language is "Receiving Gifts." If your deepest hurt is that your spouse seldom gives you quality time, then that is your primary love language.

Another approach to discovering your primary love language is to look back over your marriage and ask, "What have I most often requested of my spouse?" Whatever you have most requested is probably in keeping with your primary love language. Those requests have probably been interpreted by your spouse as nagging. They have been, in fact, your efforts to secure emotional love from your spouse.

Elizabeth, who lived in Maryville, Indiana, used that approach in discovering her primary love language. She said to me at the conclusion of a seminar session, "Whenever I look back over the last ten years of my marriage and ask myself what have I most requested of Peter, my love language becomes obvious. I have requested 'Quality Time' most often. Over and over again, I have asked him if we could go on a picnic, take a weekend together away, shut the TV off for just an hour and talk with each other, take a walk together, and on and on. I have felt neglected and unloved because seldom did he ever respond to my request. He gave me nice gifts for my birthday and special occasions and wondered why I was not excited about them.

"During your seminar," she continued, "the lights came on for both of us. During the break, my husband apologized for being so dense through the years and so resistant to my requests. He has promised me that things will be different in the future, and I believe they will."

Another way to discover your primary love language is to examine what you do or say to express love to your spouse. Chances are what you are doing for her is what you wish she would do for you. If you are constantly doing "Acts of Service" for your spouse, perhaps (although not always) that is your love language. If "Words of Affirmation" speak love to you, chances are you will use them in speaking love to your spouse. Thus, you may discover your own language by asking, "How do I consciously express my love to my spouse?"

Spend some time writing down what you think is your primary love language. Then list the other four in order of importance.

But remember, that approach is only a possible clue to your love language; it is not an absolute indicator. For example, the husband who learned from his father to express love to his wife by giving her nice gifts expresses his love to his wife by doing what his father did, yet "Receiving Gifts" is not his primary love language. He is simply doing what he was trained to do by his father.

I have suggested three ways to discover your own primary love language.

1. What does your spouse do or fail to do that hurts you most deeply? The opposite of what hurts you most is probably your love language.

2. What have you most often requested of your spouse? The thing you have most often requested is likely the thing that would make you feel most loved.

3. In what way do you regularly express love to your spouse? Your method of expressing love may be an indication that that would also make you feel loved.

Using those three approaches will probably enable you to determine your primary love language. If two languages seem to be equal for you, that is, both speak loudly to you, then perhaps you are bilingual. If so, you make it easier on your spouse. Now he or she has two choices, either of which will strongly communicate love to you.

Two kinds of people may have difficulty discovering their primary love language. The first is the individual whose emotional love tank has been full for a long time. Her spouse has expressed love in many ways, and she is not certain which of those ways makes her feel most loved. She simply knows that she is loved. The second is the individual whose love tank has been empty for so long that he doesn't remember what makes him feel loved. In either case, go back to the experience of falling in love and ask yourself, "What did I like about my spouse in those days? What did he do or say that made me desire to be with him?" If you can conjure up those memories, it will give you some idea of your primary love language. Another approach would be to ask yourself, "What would be an ideal spouse to me? If I could have the perfect mate, what would she be like?" Your picture of a perfect mate should give you some idea of your primary love language.

Having said all of that, let me suggest that you spend some time writing down what you think is your primary love language. Then list the other four in order of importance. Also write down what you think is the primary love language of your spouse. You may also list the other four in order of importance if you wish. Sit down with your spouse and discuss what you guessed to be his/her primary love language. Then tell each other what you consider to be your own primary love language.

Once you have shared that information, I suggest that you play the following game three times a week for three weeks. The game is called "Tank Check," and it is played like this. When you come home, one of you says to the other, "On a scale of zero to ten, how is your love tank tonight?" Zero means empty, and 10 means "I am full of love and can't handle any more." You give a reading on your emotional love tank—10, 9, 8, 7, 6, 5, 4, 3, 2, 1, or 0, indicating how full it is. Your spouse says, "What could I do to help fill it?"

Then you make a suggestion—something you would like your spouse to do or say that evening. To the best of his ability, he will respond to your request. Then you repeat the process in the reverse order so that both of you have the opportunity to do a reading on your love tank and to make a suggestion toward filling it. If you play the game for three weeks, you will be hooked on it, and it can be a playful way of stimulating love expressions in your marriage.

One husband said to me, "I don't like that love tank game. I played it with my wife. I came home and said to her, 'On a scale of zero to ten, how's your love tank tonight?' She said, 'About seven.' I asked, 'What could I do to help fill it?' She said, 'The greatest thing you could do for me tonight is to do the laundry.' I said, 'Love and laundry? I don't get it.'"

I said, "That's the problem. Perhaps you don't understand your wife's love language. What's your primary love language?"

Without hesitation he said, "Physical touch, and especially the sexual part of the marriage."

"Listen to me carefully," I said. "The love you feel when your wife expresses love by physical touch is the same love your wife feels when you do the laundry."

"Bring on the laundry," he shouted. "I'll wash the clothes every night if it makes her feel that good."

Incidentally, if you have still not discovered your primary love language, keep records on the tank check game. When your spouse says, "What could I do to help fill your tank?" your suggestions will likely cluster around your primary love language. You may request things from all five love languages, but you will have more requests centering on your primary love language.

Perhaps some of you are saying in your minds what Raymond and Helen said to me in Zion, Illinois. "Dr. Chapman, all that sounds fine and wonderful, but what if the love language of your spouse is something that just doesn't come naturally for you?"

I'll discuss my answer in chapter 10.

THE FIVE LOVE LANGUAGES

Love Is a Choice

LOVE IS A CHOICE

How can we speak each other's love language when we are full of hurt, anger, and resentment over past failures? The answer to that question lies in the essential nature of our humanity. We are creatures of choice. That means that we have the capacity to make poor choices, which all of us have done. We have spoken critical words, and we have done hurtful things. We are not proud of those choices, although they may have seemed justified at the moment. Poor choices in the past don't mean that we must make them in the future. Instead we can say, "I'm sorry. I know I have hurt you, but I would like to make the future different. I would like to love you in your language. I would like to meet your needs."

I have seen marriages rescued from the brink of divorce when couples make the choice to love.

THE CROCUS: "Cheerfulness, youthful gladness."

Love doesn't erase the past, but it makes the future different. When we choose active expressions of love in the primary love language of our spouse, we create an emotional climate where we can deal with our past conflicts and failures.

Brent was in my office, stone-faced and unfeeling. He had come, not by his own initiative, but at my request. A week earlier his wife, Becky, had been sitting in the same chair, weeping uncontrollably. Between her outbursts of tears, she managed to verbalize that Brent had told her that he no longer loved her and that he was leaving. She was devastated.

When she regained her composure she said, "We have both worked so hard the last two or three years. I knew that we were not spending as much time together as we used to, but I thought we were working for a common goal. I cannot believe what he is saying. He has always been such a kind and caring person. He is such a good father to our children." She continued, "How could he do this to us?"

I listened as she described their twelve years of marriage. It was a story I had heard many times before. They had an exciting courtship, got married at the height of the "in love experience," had the typical adjustments in the early days of marriage, and pursued the American dream. In due time, they came down off the emotional high of the "in love experience" but did not learn to speak each other's love language sufficiently. She had lived with a love tank only half full for the last several years, but she had received enough expressions of love to make her think that everything was OK. However, his love tank was empty.

I told Becky that I would see if Brent would talk with me. I told Brent on the phone, "As you know, Becky came to see me and told me about her struggle with what is happening in the marriage. I want to help her, but in order to do so, I need to know what you are thinking."

He agreed without hesitation, and now he sat in my office. His outward appearance was in stark contrast to Becky's. She had been weeping uncontrollably, but he was stoic. I had the impression, however, that his weeping had taken place weeks or perhaps months ago and that it had been an inward weeping. The story Brent told confirmed my hunch.

"I just don't love her anymore," he said. "I haven't loved her for a long time. I don't want to hurt her, but we are not close. Our relationship has become empty. I don't enjoy being with her anymore. I don't know what happened. I wish it were different, but I don't have any feelings for her."

Brent was thinking and feeling what hundreds of thousands of husbands have thought and felt through the years. It's the "I don't love her anymore" mind-set that gives men the emotional freedom to seek love with someone else. The same is true for wives who use the same excuse.

I sympathized with Brent, for I have been there. Thousands of husbands and wives have been there—emotionally empty, wanting to do the right thing, not wanting to hurt anyone, but being pushed by their emotional needs to seek love outside the marriage. Fortunately, I had discovered in the earlier years of my own marriage the difference between the "in love experience" and the "emotional need" to feel loved. Most in our society have not yet learned that difference. The movies, the "soaps," and the romantic magazines have intertwined these two loves, thus adding to our confusion, but they are, in fact, quite distinct.

The "in love experience" that we discussed in chapter 3 is on the level of instinct. It is not premeditated; it simply happens in the normal context of male-female relationships. It can be fostered or quenched, but it does not arise by conscious choice. It is short-lived (usually two years or less) and seems to serve for humankind the same function as the mating call of the Canada geese.

The "in love experience" temporarily meets one's emotional need for love. It gives us the feeling that someone cares, that someone admires us and appreciates us. Our emotions soar with the thought that another person sees us as number one, that he or she is willing to devote time and energies exclusively to our relationship. For a brief period, however long it lasts, our emotional need for love is met. Our tank is full; we can conquer the world. Nothing is impossible. For many individuals, it is the first time they have ever lived with a full emotional tank, and it is euphoric.

In time, however, we come down from that natural high back to the real world. If our spouse has learned to speak our primary love language, our need for love will continue to be satisfied. If, on the other hand, he or she does not speak our love language, our

Meeting my wife's need for love is a choice I make each day. If I know her primary love language and choose to speak it, her deepest emotional need will be met and she will feel secure in my love.

tank will slowly drain, and we will no longer feel loved. Meeting that need in one's spouse is definitely a choice. If I learn the emotional love language of my spouse and speak it frequently, she will continue to feel loved. When she comes down from the obsession of the "in love experience," she will hardly even miss it because her emotional love tank will continue to be filled. However, if I have not learned her primary love language or have chosen not to speak it, when she descends from the emotional high, she will have the natural yearnings of unmet emotional need. After some years of living with an empty love tank, she will likely "fall in love" with someone else and the cycle will begin again.

Meeting my wife's need for love is a choice I make each day. If I know her primary love language and choose to speak it, her deepest emotional need will be met and she will feel secure in my love. If she does the same for me, my emotional needs are met and both of us live with a full tank. In a state of emotional contentment, both of us will give our creative energies to many wholesome projects outside the marriage while we continue to keep our marriage exciting and growing.

With all of that in my mind, I looked back at the deadpan face of Brent and wondered if I could help him. I knew in my heart that he was probably already involved with another "in love experience." I wondered if it was in the beginning stages or at its height. Few men, suffering from an empty emotional love tank, leave their marriage until they have prospects of meeting that need somewhere else.

Brent was honest and revealed that he had been in love with someone else for several months. He had hoped that the feelings would go away and that he could work things out with his wife. But things at home had gotten worse, and his love for the other woman had increased. He could not imagine living without his new lover.

I sympathized with Brent in his dilemma. He sincerely did not want to hurt his wife or his children, but at the same time, he felt he deserved a life of happiness. I told him the statistics on second marriages (60 percent ending in divorce). He was surprised to hear that but was certain that he would beat the odds. I told him about the research on the effects of divorce on children, but he was convinced that he would continue to be a good father to his children and that they would get over the trauma of the divorce. I talked to Brent about the issues in this book and explained the difference between the experience of falling in love and the deep emotional need to feel loved. I explained the five love languages and challenged him to give his marriage another chance. All the while, I knew that my intellectual and reasoned approach to marriage compared to the emotional high that he was experiencing was like pitting a BB gun against an automatic weapon. He expressed appreciation for my concern and asked that I do everything possible to help Becky. But he assured me that he saw no hope for the marriage.

One month later, I received a call from Brent. He indicated that he would like to talk with me again. This time when he entered my office he was noticeably disturbed. He was not the calm, cool man I had seen before. His lover had begun to come down off the emotional high, and she was observing things in Brent that she did not like. She was withdrawing from the relationship, and he was crushed. Tears came to his eyes as he told me how much she meant to him and how unbearable it was to experience her rejection.

I listened sympathetically for an hour before Brent ever asked for my advice. I told him how sympathetic I was to his pain and indicated that what he was experiencing was the natural emotional grief from a loss and that the grief would not go away overnight. I explained, however, that the experience was inevitable. I reminded him of the temporary nature of the "in love experience," that sooner or later, we always come down from the high to the real world. Some fall out of love before they get married; others, after they get married. He agreed that it was better now than later.

After some time, I suggested that perhaps the crisis was a good time for him and his wife to get some marriage counseling. I reminded him that true, long-lasting emotional love is a choice and that emotional love could be reborn in his marriage if he and his wife learned to love each other in the right love languages. He agreed to marriage counseling; and nine months later, Brent and Becky left my office with a reborn marriage. When I saw Brent three years later, he told me what a wonderful marriage he had and thanked me for helping him at a crucial time in his life. He told me that the grief over losing the other lover had been gone for more than two years. He smiled and said, "My tank has never been so full, and Becky is the happiest woman you are ever going to meet."

Fortunately Brent was the benefactor of what I call the disequilibrium of the "in love experience." That is, almost never do two people fall in love on the same day, and almost never do they fall out of love on the same day. You don't have to be a social scientist to discover that truth. Just listen to country and western songs. Brent's lover happened to have fallen out of love at an opportune time.

In the nine months that I counseled Brent and Becky, we worked through numerous conflicts that they had never resolved before. But the key to the rebirth of their marriage was discovering each other's primary love language and choosing to speak it frequently.

Let me return to the question I raised in chapter 9. "What if the love language of your spouse is something that doesn't come naturally for you?" I am often asked this question at my marriage seminars, and my answer is, "So?"

My wife's love language is "Acts of Service." One of the things I do for her regularly as an act of love is to vacuum the floors. Do you think that vacuuming floors comes naturally for me? My mother used to make me vacuum. All through junior high and high school, I couldn't go play ball on Saturday until I finished vacuuming the entire house. In those days, I said to myself, "When I get out of here, one thing I am not going to do: I am not going to vacuum houses. I'll get myself a wife to do that."

But I vacuum our house now, and I vacuum it regularly. And there is only one reason I vacuum our house. *Love.* You couldn't pay me enough to vacuum a house, but I do it for love. You see, when an action doesn't come naturally to you, it is a greater expression of love. My wife knows that when I vacuum the house, it's nothing but 100 percent pure, unadulterated love, and I get credit for the whole thing!

Someone says, "But, Dr. Chapman, that's different. I know that my spouse's love language is physical touch, and I am not a toucher. I never saw my mother and father hug each other. They never hugged me, Dr. Chapman. I am just not a toucher. What am I going to do?"

Do you have two hands? Can you put them together? Now, imagine that you have your spouse in the middle and pull him/her toward you. I'll bet that if you hug your spouse three thousand times, it will begin to feel more comfortable. But ultimately, comfort is not the issue. We are talking about love, and love is something you do for someone else, not something you do for yourself. Most of us do many things each day that do not come "naturally" for us. For some of us, that is getting out of bed in the morning. We go against our feelings and get out of bed. Why? Because we believe there is something worthwhile to do that day. And normally, before the day is over, we feel good about having gotten up. Our actions preceded our emotions.

When an action doesn't come naturally to you, it is a greater expression of love.

The same is true with love. We discover the primary love language of our spouse, and we choose to speak it whether or not it is natural for us. We are not claiming to have warm, excited feelings. We are simply choosing to do it for his or her benefit. We want to meet our spouse's emotional need, and we reach out to speak his love language. In so doing, his emotional love tank is filled and chances are he will reciprocate and speak our language. When he does, our emotions return, and our love tank begins to fill.

Love is a choice. And either partner can start the process today.

THE FIVE LOVE LANGUAGES

Love Makes the Difference

LOVE MAKES THE DIFFERENCE

Love is not our only emotional need. Psychologists have observed that among our basic needs are the need for security, self-worth, and significance. Love, however, interfaces with all of those.

If I feel loved by my spouse, I can relax, knowing that my lover will do me no ill. I feel secure in his/her presence. I may face many uncertainties in my vocation. I may have enemies in other areas of my life, but with my spouse I feel secure.

My sense of self-worth is fed by the fact that my spouse loves me. After all, if he/she loves me, I must be worth loving. My parents may have given me negative or mixed messages about my worth, but my spouse knows me as an adult and loves me. Her love builds my self-esteem.

THE DAISY:
"Loyal love, innocence."

The need for significance is the emotional force behind much of our behavior. Life is driven by the desire for success. We want our lives to count for something. We have our own idea of what it means to be significant, and we work hard to reach our goals. Feeling loved by a spouse enhances our sense of significance. We reason, *If someone loves me, I must have significance.*

I am significant because I stand at the apex of the created order. I have the ability to think in abstract terms, communicate my thoughts via words, and make decisions. By means of printed or recorded words, I can benefit from the thoughts of those who have preceded me. I can profit from others' experience, though they lived in a different age and culture. I experience the death of family and friends and sense that there is existence beyond the material. I discover that, in all cultures, people believe in a spiritual world. My heart tells me it is true even when my mind, trained in scientific observation, raises critical questions.

I am significant. Life has meaning. There is a higher purpose. I want to believe it, but I may not feel significant until someone expresses love to me. When my spouse lovingly invests time, energy, and effort in me, I believe that I am significant. Without love, I may spend a lifetime in search of significance, self-worth, and security. When I experience love, it impacts all of those needs positively. I am now freed to develop my potential. I am more secure in my self-worth and can now turn my efforts outward instead of being obsessed with my own needs. True love always liberates.

In the context of marriage, if we do not feel loved, our differences are magnified. We come to view each other as a threat to our happiness. We fight for self-worth and significance, and marriage becomes a battlefield rather than a haven.

Love is not the answer to everything, but it creates a climate of security in which we can seek answers to those things that bother us. In the security of love, a couple can discuss differences without condemnation. Conflicts can be resolved. Two people who are different can learn to live together in harmony. We discover how to bring out the best in each other. Those are the rewards of love.

The decision to love your spouse holds tremendous potential. Learning his/her primary love language makes that potential a reality. Love really does "make the world go round." At least it did for Jean and Norm.

They had traveled for three hours to get to my office. It was obvious that Norm did not want to be there. Jean had twisted his arm by threats of leaving him. (I do not suggest this approach, but people do not always know my suggestions before they come to see me.) They had been married for thirty-five years and had never gone to counseling before.

Jean began the conversation. "Dr. Chapman, I want you to know two things up front. First of all, we don't have any money problems. I was reading in a magazine that money is the biggest problem in marriage. That's not true for us. We both have worked through the years, the house is paid for, the cars are paid for. We don't have any money problems. Second, I want you to know that we don't argue. I hear my friends talking about the arguments they have all the time. We have never argued. I can't remember the last time we ever had an argument. Both of us agree that arguing is fruitless, so we don't argue."

As a counselor, I appreciated Jean's clearing the path. I knew that she was going to get right to the point. It was obvious that she had thought through her opening statement. She wanted to make sure we didn't get bogged down in nonproblems. She wanted to use the hour wisely.

She continued. "The problem is that I just don't feel any love coming from my husband. Life is a routine for us. We get up in the morning and go off to work. In the afternoon, he does his thing and I do my thing. We generally have dinner together, but we don't talk. He watches TV while we eat. After dinner, he piddles in the basement and then sleeps in front of the TV until I tell him it's time to go to bed. That is our schedule five days a week. On Saturday, he plays golf in the morning, works in the yard in the afternoon, and we go out to dinner with another couple on Saturday night. He talks to them, but when we get into the car to go home, the conversation is over. Once we are at home, he sleeps in front of the TV until we go to bed. On Sunday morning, we go to church. We always go to church on Sunday morning, Dr. Chapman," she emphasized.

"Then," she said, "we go out to lunch with some friends. When we get home, he sleeps in front of the TV all Sunday afternoon. We usually go back to church on Sunday night, come home, eat popcorn, and go to bed. That's our schedule every week. That's all there is to it. We are like two roommates living in the same house. There is nothing going on between us. I don't feel any love coming from him. There is no warmth, there's no emotion. It's empty, it's dead. I don't think I can go on much longer like this."

By that time, Jean was crying. I handed her a tissue and looked at Norm. His first comment was, "I don't understand her." After a brief pause, he continued. "I have done everything I know to show her that I love her, especially the last two or three years since she's been complaining about it so much. Nothing seems to help. No matter what I do, she continues to complain that she doesn't feel loved. I don't know what else to do."

I could tell that Norm was frustrated and exasperated. I inquired, "What have you been doing to show your love for Jean?"

"Well, for one thing," he said, "I get home from work before she does, so I get dinner started every night. In fact, if you want to know the truth, I have dinner almost ready when she gets home four nights a week. The other night, we go out to eat. After dinner, I wash dishes three nights a week. The other night I have a meeting, but three nights I wash the dishes after dinner is over. I do all the vacuuming because her back is bad. I do all the yard work because she is allergic to pollen. I fold the clothes when they come out of the dryer."

He went on telling me other things that he did for Jean. When he finished, I wondered, *What does this woman do?* There was almost nothing left for her.

Norm continued, "I do all those things to show her that I love her, yet she sits there and says to you what she has been saying to me for two or three years—that she doesn't feel loved. I don't know what else to do for her."

When I turned back to Jean she said, "Dr. Chapman, all of those things are fine, but I want him to sit on the couch and talk to me. We don't ever talk. We haven't talked in thirty years. He's always washing dishes, vacuuming the floor, mowing the grass. He's always doing something. I want him to sit on the couch with me and give me some time, look at me, talk to me about us, about our lives."

Jean was crying again. It was obvious to me that her primary love language was "Quality Time." She was crying for attention. She wanted to be treated as a person, not an object. Norm's busyness did not meet her emotional need. As I talked further with Norm, I discovered that he didn't feel loved either, but he wasn't talking about it. He reasoned, "If you have been married for thirty-five years and your bills are paid and you don't argue, what more can you hope for?" That's where he was. But when I said to him, "What would be an ideal wife to you? If you could have a perfect wife, what would she be like?" He looked me in the eye for the first time and asked, "Do you really want to know?"

"Yes," I said.

He sat up on the couch, folded his arms across his chest. A big smile broke on his face, and he said, "I've dreamed about this. A perfect wife would be a wife who would come home in the afternoon and fix dinner for me. I would be working in the yard, and she would call me in to eat. After dinner, she would wash the dishes. I would probably help her some, but she would take the responsibility. She would sew the buttons on my shirt when they fall off."

Jean could contain herself no longer. She turned to him and said, "I'm not believing you. You told me that you liked to cook."

"I don't mind cooking," Norm responded, "but the man asked me what would be ideal."

I knew Norm's primary love language without another word— "Acts of Service." Why do you think Norm did all of those things for Jean? Because that was his love language. In his mind, that's the way you show love: by doing things for people. The problem was that "doing things" was not Jean's primary love language. It did not mean to her emotionally what it would have meant to him if she had been doing things for him.

When the light came on in Norm's mind, the first thing he said was, "Why didn't somebody tell me this thirty years ago? I could have been sitting on the couch talking to her fifteen minutes every night instead of doing all this stuff."

He turned to Jean and said, "For the first time in my life, I finally understand what you mean when you say 'We don't talk.' I could never understand that. I thought we did talk. I always ask, 'Did you sleep well?' I thought we were talking, but now I understand. You want to sit on the couch fifteen minutes every night and look at each other and talk. Now I understand what you mean, and now I know why it is so important to you. It is your emotional love language, and we'll start tonight. I'll give you fifteen minutes on the couch every night for the rest of my life. You can count on that."

Jean turned to Norm and said, "That would be heavenly, and I don't mind fixing dinner for you. It will have to be later than usual because I get off work later than you, but I don't mind fixing dinner. And I would love to sew your buttons on. You never left them off long enough for me to get them. I'll wash dishes the rest of my life if it will make you feel loved."

Jean and Norm went home and started loving each other in the right love languages. In less than two months, they were on a second honeymoon. They called me from the Bahamas to tell me what a radical change had taken place in their marriage.

Can emotional love be reborn in a marriage? You bet. The key is to learn the primary love language of your spouse and choose to speak it.

THE FIVE LOVE LANGUAGES

Loving the Unlovely

LOVING THE UNLOVELY

I t was a beautiful September Saturday. My wife and I were strolling through Reynolda Gardens, enjoying the flora, some of which had been imported from around the world. The gardens had originally been developed by R. J. Reynolds, the tobacco magnate, as a part of his country estate. They are now a part of the Wake Forest University campus. We had just passed the rose garden when I noticed Ann, a woman who had begun counseling two weeks earlier, approaching us. She was looking down at the cobblestone walkway and appeared to be in deep thought. When I greeted her, she was startled but looked up and smiled. I introduced her to Karolyn, and we exchanged pleasantries. Then, without any lead-in, she asked me one of the most profound questions I have ever heard: "Dr. Chapman, is it possible to love someone whom you hate?"

THE WATER LILY:
"Purity of heart."

I knew the question was born of deep hurt and deserved a thoughtful answer. I knew that I would be seeing her the following week for another counseling appointment, so I said, "Ann, that is one of the most thought-provoking questions I have ever heard. Why don't we discuss that next week?" She agreed, and Karolyn and I continued our stroll. But Ann's question did not go away. Later, as we drove home, Karolyn and I discussed it. We reflected on the early days of our own marriage and remembered that we had often experienced feelings of hate. Our condemning words to each other had stimulated hurt and, on the heels of hurt, anger. Anger held inside becomes hate. What made the difference for us? We both knew it was the choice to love. We had realized that if we continued our pattern of demanding and condemning, we would destroy our marriage. Fortunately over a period of about a year, we had learned how to discuss our differences without condemning each other, how to make decisions without destroying our unity, how to give constructive suggestions without being demanding, and eventually how to speak each other's primary love language. (Many of those insights are recorded in an earlier book, *Toward a Growing Marriage*, Moody Publishers.) Our choice to love was made in the midst of negative feelings toward each other. When we started speaking each other's primary love language, the negative feelings of anger and hate abated.

Our situation, however, was different from Ann's. Karolyn and I had both been open to learning and growing. I knew that Ann's husband was not. She had told me the previous week that she had begged him to go for counseling. She had pleaded for him to read a book or listen to a tape on marriage, but he had refused all her efforts toward growth. According to her, his attitude was: "I don't have any problems. You are the one with the problems." In his mind he was right; she was wrong—it was as simple as that. Her feelings of love for him had been killed through the years by his constant criticism and condemnation. After ten years of marriage, her emotional energy was depleted and her self-esteem almost destroyed. Was there hope for Ann's marriage? Could she love an unlovely husband? Would he ever respond in love to her?

I knew that Ann was a deeply religious person and that she attended church regularly. I surmised that perhaps her only hope for marital survival was in her faith. The next day, with Ann in mind, I began to read Luke's account of the life of Christ. I have always admired Luke's writing because he was a physician who gave attention to details and in the first century wrote an orderly account of the teachings and lifestyle of Jesus of Nazareth. In what many have called Jesus' greatest sermon, I read the following words, which I call love's greatest challenge.

I tell you who hear me: Love your enemies, do good to those who hate you, bless those who curse you, pray for those who mistreat you. . . . Do to others as you would have them do to you. If you love those who love you, what credit is that to you? Even "sinners" love those who love them.[1]

It seemed to me that that profound challenge, written almost two thousand years ago, might be the direction that Ann was looking for, but could she do it? Could anyone do it? Is it possible to love a spouse who has become your enemy? Is it possible to love one who has cursed you, mistreated you, and expressed feelings of contempt and hate for you? And if she could, would there be any payback? Would her husband ever change and begin to express love and care for her? I was astounded by this further word from Jesus' ancient sermon: "Give, and it will be given to you. A good measure, pressed down, shaken together and running over, will be poured into your lap. For with the measure you use, it will be measured to you."[2]

Could that ancient principle of loving an unlovely person possibly work in a marriage as far gone as Ann's? I decided to do an experiment. I would take as my hypothesis that if Ann could learn her husband's primary love language and speak it for a period of time so that his emotional need for love was met, eventually he would reciprocate and begin to express love to her. I wondered, *Would it work?*

I met with Ann the next week and listened again as she reviewed the horrors of her marriage. At the end of her synopsis, she repeated the question she had asked in Reynolda Gardens. This time she put it in the form of a statement: "Dr. Chapman, I just don't know if I can ever love him again after all he has done to me."

"Have you talked about your situation with any of your friends?" I asked.

"With two of my closest friends," she said, "and a little bit with some other people."

"And what was their response?"

"Get out," she said. "They all tell me to get out, that he will never change, and that I am simply prolonging the agony. But, Dr. Chapman, I just can't bring myself to do that. Maybe I should, but I just can't believe that's the right thing to do."

"It seems to me that you are torn between your religious and moral beliefs that tell you it is wrong to get out of the marriage, and your emotional pain, which tells you that getting out is the only way to survive," I said.

"That's exactly right, Dr. Chapman. That's exactly the way I feel. I don't know what to do."

"I am deeply sympathetic with your struggle," I continued. "You are in a very difficult situation. I wish I could offer you an easy answer. Unfortunately, I can't. Both of the alternatives you mentioned, getting out or staying in, will likely bring you a great deal of pain. Before you make that decision, I do have one idea. I am not sure it will work, but I'd like you to try it. I know from what you have told me that your religious faith is important to you and that you have a great deal of respect for the teachings of Jesus."

She nodded affirmingly. I continued, "I want to read something that Jesus once said that I think has some application to your marriage." I read slowly and deliberately.

"'I tell you who hear me: Love your enemies, do good to those who hate you, bless those who curse you, pray for those who mistreat you. . . . Do to others as you would have them do to you. If you love those who love you, what credit is that to you? Even "sinners" love those who love them.'

"Does that sound like your husband? Has he treated you as an enemy rather than as a friend?" I inquired.

She nodded her head affirmingly.

"Has he ever cursed you?" I asked.

"Many times."

"Has he ever mistreated you?"

"Often."

"And has he told you that he hates you?"

"Yes."

"Ann, if you are willing, I would like to do an experiment. I would like to see what would happen if we apply this principle to your marriage. Let me explain what I mean." I went on to explain to Ann the concept of the emotional tank and the fact that when the tank is low, as hers was, we have no love feelings toward our spouse but simply experience emptiness and pain. Since love is such a deep emotional need, the lack of it is perhaps our deepest emotional pain. I told her that if we could learn to speak each other's primary love language, that emotional need could be met and positive feelings could be engendered again.

When the tank is low . . . we have no love feelings toward our spouse but simply experience emptiness and pain.

"Does that make sense to you?" I inquired.

"Dr. Chapman, you have just described my life. I have never seen it so clearly before. We were in love before we got married, but not long after our marriage we came down off the high and we never learned to speak each other's love language. My tank has been empty for years, and I am sure his has also. Dr. Chapman, if I had understood this concept earlier, maybe none of this would have happened."

"We can't go back, Ann," I said. "All we can do is try to make the future different. I would like to propose a six-month experiment."

"I'll try anything," Ann said.

I liked her positive spirit, but I wasn't sure whether she understood how difficult the experiment would be.

"Let's begin by stating our objective," I said. "If in six months you could have your fondest wish, what would it be?"

Ann sat in silence for some time. Then thoughtfully she said, "I would like to see Glenn loving me again and expressing it by spending time with me. I would like to see us doing things together, going places together. I would like to feel that he is interested in my world. I would like to see us talking when we go out to eat. I'd like him to listen to me. I'd like to feel that he values my ideas. I would like to see us taking trips together and having fun again. I would like to know that he values our marriage more than anything."

Ann paused and then continued. "On my part, I would like to have warm, positive feelings toward him again. I would like to gain respect for him again. I would like to be proud of him. Right now, I don't have those feelings."

I was writing as Ann was speaking. When she finished, I read aloud what she had said. "That sounds like a pretty lofty objective," I said, "but is that really what you want, Ann?"

"Right now, that sounds like an impossible objective, Dr. Chapman," Ann replied, "but more than anything, that's what I would like to see."

"Then let's agree," I said, "that this will be our objective. In six months, we want to see you and Glenn having this kind of love relationship.

"Now, let me suggest a hypothesis. The purpose of our experiment will be to prove whether or not the hypothesis is true. Let's hypothesize that if you could speak Glenn's primary love language consistently for a six-month period, that somewhere along the line his emotional need for love would begin to be met; and as his emotional tank filled, he would begin to reciprocate love to you. That hypothesis is built upon the idea that the emotional need for love is our deepest emotional need; and when that need is being met, we tend to respond positively to the person who is meeting it."

I continued, "You understand that that hypothesis places all the initiative in your hands. Glenn is not trying to work on this marriage.

You are. This hypothesis says that if you can channel your energies in the right direction, there is a good possibility that Glenn will eventually reciprocate." I read the other portion of Jesus' sermon recorded by Luke, the physician. "'Give, and it will be given to you. A good measure, pressed down, shaken together and running over, will be poured into your lap. For with the measure you use, it will be measured to you.'

"As I understand that, Jesus is stating a principle, not a way to manipulate people. Generally speaking, if we are kind and loving toward people, they will tend to be kind and loving toward us. That does not mean that we can make a person kind by being kind to him. We are independent agents. Thus, we can spurn love and walk away from love or even spit into the face of love. There is no guarantee that Glenn will respond to your acts of love. We can only say that there is a good possibility he will do so." (A counselor can never predict with absolute certainty individual human behavior. Based on research and personality studies, a counselor can only predict how a person is likely to respond in a given situation.)

After we agreed on the hypothesis, I said to Ann, "Now let's discuss your and Glenn's primary love languages. I'm assuming from what you have told me already that quality time may be your primary love language. What do you think?"

"I think so, Dr. Chapman. In the early days when we spent time together and Glenn listened to me, we spent long hours talking together, doing things together. I really felt loved. More than anything, I wish that part of our marriage could return. When we spend time together, I feel like he really cares, but when he's always doing other things, never has time to talk, never has time to do anything with me, I feel like business and other pursuits are more important than our relationship."

"And what do you think Glenn's primary love language is?" I inquired.

"I think it is physical touch and especially the sexual part of the marriage. I know that when I felt more loved by him and we were more sexually active, he had a different attitude. I think that's his primary love language, Dr. Chapman."

"Does he ever complain about the way you talk to him?"

"Well, he says I nag him all the time. He also says that I don't support him, that I'm always against his ideas."

"Then, let's assume," I said, "that 'Physical Touch' is his primary love language and 'Words of Affirmation' is his secondary love language. The reason I suggest the second is that if he complains about negative words, apparently positive words would be meaningful to him.

"Now, let me suggest a plan to test our hypothesis. What if you go home and say to Glenn, 'I've been thinking about us and I've decided that I would like to be a better wife to you. So if you have any suggestions as to how I could be a better wife, I want you to know that I am open to them. You can tell me now or you can think about it and let me know what you think, but I would really like to work on being a better wife.' Whatever his response, negative or positive, simply accept it as information. That initial statement lets him know that something different is about to happen in your relationship.

"Then based upon your guess that his primary love language is 'Physical Touch' and my suggestion that his secondary love language may be 'Words of Affirmation,' focus your attention on those two areas for one month.

"If Glenn comes back with a suggestion as to how you might be a better wife, accept that information and work it into your plan. Look for positive things in Glenn's life and give him verbal affirmation about those things. In the meantime, stop all verbal complaints. If you want to complain about something, write it down in your personal notebook rather than saying anything about it to Glenn this month.

"Begin taking more initiative in physical touch and sexual involvement. Surprise him by being aggressive, not simply responding to his advances. Set a goal to have sexual intercourse at least once a week the first two weeks and twice a week the following two weeks." Ann had told me that she and Glenn had had sexual intercourse only once or twice in the past six months. I figured this plan would get things off dead center rather quickly.

"Oh, Dr. Chapman, this is going to be difficult," Ann said. "I have found it hard to be sexually responsive to him when he ignores me all the time. I have felt used rather than loved in our sexual encounters. He acts as though I am totally unimportant all the rest of the time and then wants to jump in bed and use my body. I have resented that, and I guess that's why we have not had sex very often in the last few years."

"Your response has been natural and normal," I assured Ann. "For most wives, the desire to be sexually intimate with their husbands grows out of a sense of being loved by their husbands. If they feel loved, then they desire sexual intimacy. If they do not feel loved, they likely feel used in the sexual context. That is why loving someone who is not loving you is extremely difficult. It goes against our natural tendencies. You will probably have to rely heavily upon your faith in God in order to do this. Perhaps it will help if you read again Jesus' sermon on loving your enemies, loving those who hate you, loving those who use you. And then ask God to help you practice the teachings of Jesus."

I could tell that Ann was following what I was saying. Her head was nodding ever so slightly. Her eyes told me she had lots of questions.

If you claim to have feelings that you do not have, that is hypocritical. . . . But if you express an act of love that is designed for the other person's benefit or pleasure, it is simply a choice.

"But, Dr. Chapman, isn't it being hypocritical to express love sexually when you have such negative feelings toward the person?"

"Perhaps it would be helpful for us to distinguish between love as a feeling and love as an action," I said. "If you claim to have feelings that you do not have, that is hypocritical and such false communication is not the way to build intimate relationships. But if you express an act of love that is designed for the other person's benefit or pleasure, it is simply a choice. You are not claiming that the action grows out of a deep emotional bonding. You are simply choosing to do something for his benefit. I think that must be what Jesus meant.

"Certainly we do not have warm feelings for people who hate us. That would be abnormal, but we can do loving acts for them. That is simply a choice. We hope that such loving acts will have a positive effect upon their attitudes and behavior and treatment, but at least we have chosen to do something positive for them."

My answer seemed to satisfy Ann, at least for the moment. I had the feeling that we would discuss that again. I also had the feeling that if the experiment was going to get off the ground, it would be because of Ann's deep faith in God.

"After the first month," I said, "I want you to ask Glenn for feedback on how you are doing. Using your own words, ask him, 'Glenn, you remember a few weeks ago when I told you I was going to try to be a better wife? I want to ask how you think I am doing.'

"Whatever Glenn says, accept it as information. He may be sarcastic, he may be flippant or hostile, or he may be positive. Whatever his response, do not argue but accept it and assure him that you are serious and that you really want to be a better wife, and if he has additional suggestions, you are open to them.

"Follow this pattern of asking for feedback once a month for the entire six months. Whenever Glenn gives you the first positive feedback, whenever he says, 'You know, I have to admit that when you first told me that you were going to try to be better, I pretty much laughed it off, but I'll have to acknowledge that things are different around here,' you will know that your efforts are getting through to him emotionally. He may give you positive feedback after the first month, or it may be after the second or third. One week after you receive the first positive feedback, I want you to make a request of Glenn—something that you would like him to do, something in keeping with your primary love language. For example, you may say to him one evening, 'Glenn, do you know something I would like to do? Do you remember how we used to play Scrabble together? I'd like to play Scrabble with you on Thursday night. The kids are going to be staying at Mary's. Do you think that would be possible?'

"Make the request something specific, not general. Don't say, 'You know, I wish we would spend more time together.' That's too vague. How will you know when he's done it? But if you make your request specific, he will know exactly what you want and you will know that, when he does it, he is choosing to do something for your benefit.

Perhaps you need a miracle in your own marriage. Why not try Ann's experiment?

"Make a specific request of him each month. If he does it, fine; if he doesn't do it, fine. But when he does it, you will know that he is responding to your needs. In the process, you are teaching him your primary love language because the requests you make are in keeping with your love language. If he chooses to begin loving you in your primary language, your positive emotions toward him will begin to resurface. Your emotional tank will begin to fill up and in time the marriage will, in fact, be reborn."

"Dr. Chapman, I would do anything if that could happen," Ann said.

"Well," I responded, "it will take a lot of hard work, but I believe it's worth a try. I'm personally interested to see if this experiment works and if our hypothesis is true. I would like to meet with you regularly throughout this process—perhaps every two weeks—and I would like you to keep records on the positive words of affirmation that you give Glenn each week. Also, I would like you to bring me your list of complaints that you have written in your notebook without stating them to Glenn. Perhaps from the felt complaints, I can help you build specific requests for Glenn that will help meet some of those frustrations. Eventually, I want you to learn how to share your frustrations and irritations in a constructive way, and I want you and Glenn to learn how to work through those irritations and conflicts. But during this six-month experiment, I want you to write them down without telling Glenn."

Ann left, and I believed that she had the answer to her question: "Is it possible to love someone whom you hate?"

In the next six months, Ann saw a tremendous change in Glenn's attitude and treatment of her. The first month, he was flippant and treated the whole thing lightly. But after the second month, he gave her positive feedback about her efforts. In the last four months, he responded positively to almost all of her requests, and her feelings for him began to change drastically. Glenn never came for counseling, but he did listen to some of my tapes and discuss them with Ann. He encouraged Ann to continue her counseling, which she did for another three months after our experiment. To this day, Glenn swears to his friends that I am a miracle worker. I know in fact that love is a miracle worker.

Perhaps you need a miracle in your own marriage. Why not try Ann's experiment? Tell your spouse that you have been thinking about your marriage and have decided that you would like to do a better job of meeting his/her needs. Ask for suggestions on how you could improve. His suggestions will be a clue to his primary love language. If he makes no suggestions, guess his love language based on the things he has complained about over the years. Then, for six months, focus your attention on that love language. At the end of each month, ask your spouse for feedback on how you are doing and for further suggestions.

Whenever your spouse indicates that he is seeing improvement, wait one week and then make a specific request. The request should be something you really want him to do for you. If he chooses to do it, you will know that he is responding to your needs. If he does not honor your request, continue to love him. Maybe next month he will respond positively. If your spouse starts speaking your love language by responding to your requests, your positive emotions toward him will return, and in time your marriage will be reborn. I cannot guarantee the results, but scores of people whom I have counseled have experienced the miracle of love.

NOTES
1. Luke 6:27–28, 31–32.
2. Luke 6:38.

THE FIVE LOVE LANGUAGES

Children and Love Languages

CHILDREN AND LOVE LANGUAGES

Does the concept of love languages apply to children? I am often asked that question by those attending my marriage seminars. My unqualified answer is yes. When children are little, you don't know their primary love language. Therefore, pour on all five and you are bound to hit it; but if you observe their behavior, you can learn their primary love language rather early.

Bobby is six years old. When his father comes home from work, Bobby jumps into his lap, reaches up, and messes up his father's hair. What is Bobby saying to his father? "I want to be touched." He is touching his father because he wants to be touched. Bobby's primary love language is likely "Physical Touch."

Patrick lives next door to Bobby. He is five and a half, and he and Bobby are playmates. Patrick's father, however, faces a different scenario when he comes home from work. Patrick says excitedly, "Come here, Daddy. I want to show you something. Come here."

THE MORNING GLORY: "Affection."

His father says, "Just a minute, Patrick, I want to look at the paper."

Patrick leaves for a moment but is back in fifteen seconds, saying, "Daddy, come to my room. I want to show you now, Daddy. I want to show you now."

His father replies, "Just a minute, son. Let me finish reading."

Patrick's mother calls him, and he dashes off. His mother tells him that his father is tired and please let him read the paper for a few minutes. Patrick says, "But, Mommy, I want to show him what I made."

"I know," says his mother, "but let Dad read for a few minutes."

Sixty seconds later, Patrick is back to his father and instead of saying anything, he jumps into his father's paper, laughing. His father says, "What are you doing, Patrick?"

Patrick says, "I want you to come to my room, Daddy. I want to show you what I made."

What is Patrick requesting? "Quality Time." He wants his father's undivided attention, and he won't stop until he gets it, even if he must create a scene.

If your child is often making presents for you, wrapping them up and giving them to you with a special glee in his or her eye, your child's primary love language is probably "Receiving Gifts." He gives to you because he desires to receive. If you observe your son or daughter always trying to help a younger brother or sister, it probably means that his or her primary love language is "Acts of Service." If he or she is often telling you how good you look and what a good mother or father you are and what a good job you did, it is an indicator that his or her primary love language is "Words of Affirmation."

All of that is on the subconscious level for the child. That is, the child is not consciously thinking, "If I give a gift, my parents will give me a gift; if I touch, I will be touched," but her behavior is motivated by her own emotional desires. Perhaps she has learned by experience that when she does or says certain things, she typically receives certain responses from her parents. Thus, she does or says that which results in getting her own emotional needs met. If all goes well and their emotional needs are met, children develop into responsible adults; but if the emotional need is not met, they may violate acceptable standards, expressing anger toward parents who did not meet their needs, and seeking love in inappropriate places.

Dr. Ross Campbell, the psychiatrist who first told me about the emotional love tank, says that in his many years of treating adolescents who have been involved in sexual misconduct, he has never treated such an adolescent whose emotional need for love has been met by the parents. His opinion was that almost all sexual misconduct in adolescents is rooted in an empty emotional love tank.

Have you seen that in your community? A teenager runs away from home. The parents wring their hands, saying, "How could he do this to us after all we have done for him?" but the teenager is sixty miles down the road in some counselor's office, saying, "My parents don't love me. They have never loved me. They love my brother, but they don't love me." Do the parents, in fact, love that teenager? In the majority of cases, they do. Then what's the problem? Very likely, the parents never learned how to communicate love in a language the child could understand.

Perhaps they bought ball gloves and bicycles to show their love, but the child was crying, "Will someone play ball with me? Will someone go riding with me?" The difference between buying a ball glove and playing ball with a child may be the difference between an empty love tank and a full one. Parents can sincerely love their children (most do), but sincerity is not enough. We must learn to speak the primary love language of our children if we are to meet their emotional need for love.

Let's look at the five love languages in the context of loving children.

Why is it that as the child gets older, our "Words of Affirmation" turn to words of condemnation?

Words of Affirmation

Parents typically give many affirming words when the child is young. Even before the child understands verbal communication, parents are saying, "What a pretty nose, what beautiful eyes, what curly hair," and so on. When the child begins to crawl, we applaud every movement and give "Words of Affirmation." When he begins to walk and stands with one hand against the couch, we stand two feet away and say, "Come on, come on, come on. That's right! Walk. That's right, walk." The child takes half a step and falls and what do we say? We don't say, "You dumb kid, can't you walk?" Rather, we say, "Yea, good job!" So he gets up and tries again.

Why is it that as the child gets older, our "Words of Affirmation" turn to words of condemnation? When the child is seven we walk into the room and tell him to put the toys in the toy box. Twelve toys are on the floor. We come back in five minutes and seven toys are in the box, and what do we say? "I told you to get these toys up. If you don't get these toys up, I am going to—" What about the seven toys in the box? Why don't we say, "Yea, Johnny, you put seven toys in the box. That's great." The other five would probably jump into the box! As the child gets older, we tend to condemn him for his failures rather than commend him for his successes.

To a child whose primary love language is "Words of Affirmation," our negative, critical, demeaning words strike terror to her psyche. Hundreds of thirty-five-year-old adults still hear words of condemnation spoken twenty years ago ringing in their ears: "You're too fat; nobody will ever date you." "You're not a student. You may as well drop out of school." "I can't believe you are so dumb." "You are irresponsible and will never amount to anything." Adults struggle with self-esteem and feel unloved all their lives when their primary love language is violated in such a detrimental manner.

Quality Time

Quality time means giving a child undivided attention. For the small child, it means sitting on the floor and rolling a ball back and forth with him. We are talking about playing with cars or dolls. We are talking about playing in the sandbox and building castles, getting into his world, doing things with him. You may be into computers as an adult, but your child lives in a child's world. You must get down on the child's level if you eventually want to lead him to the adult world.

As the child gets older and develops new interests, you must enter into those interests if you want to meet his needs. If he is into basket-ball, get interested in basketball, spend time playing basketball with him, take him to basketball games. If he is into piano, perhaps you could take a piano lesson or at least listen with undivided attention for part of his practice period. Giving a child your undivided attention says that you care, that he is important to you, that you enjoy being with him.

Many adults, looking back on childhood, do not remember much of what their parents said, but they do remember what their parents did. One adult said, "I remember that my father never missed my high school games. I knew he was interested in what I was doing." For that adult, "Quality Time" was an extremely important communicator of love. If "Quality Time" is the primary love language of your child and you speak that language, chances are he will allow you to spend quality time with him even through the adolescent years. If you do not give him quality time in the younger years, he will likely seek the attention of peers during the adolescent years and turn away from parents who may at that time desperately desire more time with their children.

Receiving Gifts

Many parents and grandparents speak the language of gifts excessively. In fact, when one visits toy stores, one wonders if parents believe that is the only language of love. If parents have the money, they tend to buy many gifts for their children. Some parents believe that that is the best way to show love. Some parents try to do for their children what their parents were unable to do for them. They buy things that they wish they had had as a child. But unless that is the primary love language of the child, gifts may mean little emotionally to the child. The parent has good intentions, but he/she is not meeting the emotional needs of the child by giving gifts.

If the gifts you give are quickly laid aside, if the child seldom says "thank you," if the child does not take care of the gifts that you have given, if she does not prize those gifts, chances are "Receiving Gifts" is not her primary love language. If, on the other hand, your child responds to you with much thanksgiving, if she shows others the gift and tells others how wonderful you are for buying the gift, if she takes care of the gift, if she puts it in a place of prominence in her room and keeps it polished, if she plays with it often over an extended period of time, then perhaps "Receiving Gifts" is her primary love language.

What if you have a child for whom "Receiving Gifts" is his or her primary love language but you cannot afford many gifts? Remember, it's not the quality or cost of the gift; it is the "thought that counts." Many gifts can be handmade, and sometimes the child appreciates that gift more than an expensive, manufactured gift. In fact, younger children will often play with a box more than the toy that came in it. You can also find discarded toys and refinish them. The process of refinishing can become a project for both parent and child. You need not have lots of money in order to provide gifts for your children.

Acts of Service

When children are small, parents are continually doing "Acts of Service" for them. If they did not, the child would die. Bathing, feeding, and dressing all require a great deal of work in the first few years of a child's life. Then comes cooking, washing, and ironing. Then comes packing lunches, running a taxi service, and helping with homework. Such things are taken for granted by many children, but for other children those things communicate love.

If your child is often expressing appreciation for ordinary acts of service, that is a clue that they are emotionally important to him or her. Your acts of service are communicating love in a meaningful way. When you help him with a science project, it means more than a good grade. It means "My parent loves me." When you fix a bicycle, you do more than get him back on wheels. You send him away with a full tank. If your child consistently offers to help you with your work projects, it probably means that in his mind that is a way of expressing love, and "Acts of Service" likely is his primary love language.

Physical Touch

We have long known that "Physical Touch" is an emotional communicator to children. Research has shown that babies who are handled often develop better emotionally than babies who are not. Naturally many parents and other adults pick up an infant, hold it, cuddle it, kiss it, squeeze it, and speak silly words to it. Long before the child understands the meaning of the word *love*, she feels loved. Hugging, kissing, patting, holding hands are all ways of communicating love to a child. The hugging and kissing of a teenager will differ from the hugging and kissing of an infant. Your teenager may not appreciate such behavior in the presence of peers, but that doesn't mean that he does not want to be touched, especially if it is his primary love language.

If your teenager is regularly coming up behind you and grabbing your arms, lightly pushing you, grabbing you by the ankle when you walk through the room, tripping you, those are all indications that "Physical Touch" is important to him.

Observe your children. Watch how they express love to others. That is a clue to their love language. Take note of the things they request of you. Many times, their request will be in keeping with their own love language. Notice the things for which they are most appreciative. Those are likely indicators of their primary love language.

Our daughter's love language is "Quality Time"; thus, as she grew up, she and I often took walks together. During her high school years while she attended Salem Academy, one of the oldest girls' academies

Observe your children. Watch how they express love to others. That is a clue to their love language.

in the country, we took walks amid the quaint surroundings of Old Salem. The Moravians have restored the village, which is more than two hundred years old. Walking the cobblestone streets takes one back to a simpler time. Strolling through the ancient cemetery gives one a sense of reality about life and death. In those years, we walked three afternoons a week and had long discussions in that austere setting. She is a medical doctor now, but when she comes home, she almost always says, "Want to take a walk, Dad?" I have never refused her invitation.

My son would never walk with me. He said, "Walking's dumb! You're not going anywhere. If you're going somewhere, drive."

"Quality Time" was not his primary love language. As parents, we often try to pour all of our children into the same mold. We go to parenting conferences or read books on parenting, get some wonderful ideas, and want to go home and practice with each child. The problem is that each child is different, and what communicates love to one child may not communicate love to another. Forcing a child to take a walk with you so that you can spend quality time together will not communicate love. We must learn to speak our children's language if we want them to feel loved.

I believe that most parents sincerely love their children. I also believe that thousands of parents have failed to communicate love in the proper language and thousands of children in this country are living with an empty emotional tank. I believe that most misbehavior in children and teenagers can be traced to empty love tanks.

It is never too late to express love. If you have older children and realize that you have been speaking the wrong love language, why not tell them? "You know, I have been reading a book on how to express love, and I realize that I have not been expressing my love to you in the best way through the years. I have tried to show you my love by _____, but I'm now realizing that that probably has not communicated love to you, that your love language is probably something different. I am beginning to think that your love language is probably

_____. You know, I really do love you, and I hope that in the future I can express it to you in better ways." You might even want to explain the five love languages to them and discuss your love language as well as theirs.

Perhaps you do not feel loved by your older children. If they are old enough to understand the concept of love languages, your discussion may open their eyes. You may be surprised at their willingness to start speaking your love language and, if they do, you might be surprised at the way your feelings and attitudes toward them begin to change. When family members start speaking each other's primary love language, the emotional climate of a family is greatly enhanced.

THE FIVE LOVE LANGUAGES

A Personal Word

A PERSONAL WORD

In chapter 2, I warned the reader that "understanding the five love languages and learning to speak the primary love language of your spouse may radically affect his or her behavior." Now I ask, "What do you think?" Having read these pages, walked in and out of the lives of several couples, visited small villages and large cities, sat with me in the counseling office, and talked with people in restaurants, what do you think? Could these concepts radically alter the emotional climate of your marriage? What would happen if you discovered the primary love language of your spouse and chose to speak it consistently?

Neither you nor I can answer that question until you have tried it. I know that many couples who have heard this concept at my marriage seminars say that choosing to love and expressing it in the primary love language of their spouse has made a drastic difference in their marriage. When the emotional need for love is met, it creates a climate where the couple can deal with the rest of life in a much more productive manner.

A YELLOW LILY: "Walking on air, gaiety."

We each come to marriage with a different personality and history. We bring emotional baggage into our marriage relationship. We come with different expectations, different ways of approaching things, and different opinions about what matters in life. In a healthy marriage, that variety of perspectives must be processed. We need not agree on everything, but we must find a way to handle our differences so that they do not become divisive. With empty love tanks, couples tend to argue and withdraw, and some may tend to be violent verbally or physically in their arguments. But when the love tank is full, we create a climate of friendliness, a climate that seeks to understand, that is willing to allow differences and to negotiate problems. I am convinced that no single area of marriage affects the rest of marriage as much as meeting the emotional need for love.

The ability to love, especially when your spouse is not loving you, may seem impossible for some. Such love may require us to draw upon our spiritual resources. A number of years ago, as I faced my own marital struggles, I rediscovered my need for God. As an anthropologist, I had been trained to examine data. I decided to personally excavate the roots of the Christian faith. Examining the historical accounts of Christ's birth, life, death, and resurrection, I came to view His death as an expression of love and His resurrection as profound evidence of His power. I became a true "believer." I committed my life to Him and have found that He provides the inner spiritual energy to love, even when love is not reciprocated. I would encourage you to make your own investigation of the one whom, as He died, prayed for those who killed Him: "Father, forgive them for they know not what they do." That is love's ultimate expression.

The high divorce rate in our country bears witness that thousands of married couples have been living with an empty emotional love tank. The growing number of adolescents who run away from home and clash with the law indicates that many parents who may have sincerely tried to express love to their children have been speaking the wrong love language. I believe that the concepts in this book could make an impact upon the marriages and families of our country.

I have not written this book as an academic treatise to be stored in the libraries of colleges and universities, although I hope that professors of sociology and psychology will find it helpful in courses on marriage and family life. I have written not to those who are studying marriage but to those who are married, to those who have experienced the "in love" euphoria, who entered marriage with lofty dreams of making each other supremely happy but in the reality of day-to-day life are in danger of losing that dream entirely. It is my hope that thousands of those couples will not only rediscover their dream but will see the path to making their dreams come true.

I dream of a day when the potential of the married couples in this country can be unleashed for the good of humankind, when husbands and wives can live life with full emotional love tanks and reach out to accomplish their potential as individuals and as couples. I dream of a day when children can grow up in homes filled with love and security, where children's developing energies can be channeled to learning and serving rather than seeking the love they did not receive at home. It is my desire that this brief volume will kindle the flame of love in your marriage and in the marriages of thousands of other couples like you.

If it were possible, I would hand this book personally to every married couple in this country and say, "I wrote this for you. I hope it changes your life. And if it does, be sure to give it to someone else." Since I cannot do that, I would be pleased if you would give a copy of this book to your family, to your brothers and sisters, to your married children, to your employees, to those in your civic club or church or synagogue. Who knows, together we may see our dream come true.

For a free on-line study guide please visit:

http://www.fivelovelanguages.com

The study guide was designed to take the concepts from *The Five Love Languages* book and teach you how to apply them to your life in a practical way. There is one page of study notes per chapter. For couple or group studies and discussion groups.

PROFILE FOR HUSBANDS

You may think you already know your primary love language. Then again, you may have no clue. The Five Love Languages Profile will help you know for certain which love language is yours —Words of Affirmation, Quality Time, Receiving Gifts, Acts of Service, or Physical Touch.

The profile consists of 30 pairs of statements. You can only pick one statement in each pair as the one that best represents your desire. Read each pair of statements, and then, in the right-hand column, circle the letter that matches up with the statement you choose. It may be tough at times to decide between two statements, but you should only choose one per pair to ensure the most accurate profile results.

Allow at least 15 to 30 minutes to complete the profile. Take it when you are relaxed, and try not to rush through it. Once you've made your selections, go back and count the number of times you circled each individual letter. You can list the results in the appropriate spaces at the end of the profile.

| 1 | My wife's love notes make me feel good. | A |
| | I love my wife's hugs. | E |

| 2 | I like to be alone with my wife. | B |
| | I feel loved when my wife helps me do yard work. | D |

| 3 | Receiving special gifts from my wife makes me happy. | C |
| | I enjoy long trips with my wife. | B |

| 4 | I feel loved when my wife does my laundry. | D |
| | I like it when my wife touches me. | E |

| 5 | I feel loved when my wife puts her arm around me. | E |
| | I know my wife loves me because she surprises me with gifts. | C |

| 6 | I like going most anywhere with my wife. | B |
| | I like to hold my wife's hand. | E |

| 7 | I value the gifts my wife gives to me. | C |
| | I love to hear my wife say she loves me. | A |

| 8 | I like for my wife to sit close to me. | E |
| | My wife tells me I look good, and I like that. | A |

| 9 | Spending time with my wife makes me happy. | B |
| | Even the smallest gift from my wife is important to me. | C |

| 10 | I feel loved when my wife tells me she is proud of me. | A |
| | When my wife cooks a meal for me, I know that she loves me. | D |

| 11 | No matter what we do, I love doing things with my wife. | B |
| | Supportive comments from my wife make me feel good. | A |

| 12 | Little things my wife does for me mean more to me than things she says. | D |
| | I love to hug my wife. | E |

| 13 | My wife's praise means a lot to me. | A |
| | It means a lot to me that my wife gives me gifts I really like. | C |

| 14 | Just being around my wife makes me feel good. | B |
| | I love it when my wife rubs my back. | E |

| 15 | My wife's reactions to my accomplishments are so encouraging. | A |
| | It means a lot to me when my wife helps with something I know she hates. | D |

| 16 | I never get tired of my wife's kisses. | E |
| | I love that my wife shows real interest in things I like to do. | B |

| 17 | I can count on my wife to help me with projects. | D |
| | I still get excited when opening a gift from my wife. | C |

| 18 | I love for my wife to compliment my appearance. | A |
| | I love that my wife listens to my ideas and doesn't rush to judge or criticize. | B |

| 19 | I can't help but touch my wife when she's close by. | E |
| | My wife sometimes runs errands for me, and I appreciate that. | D |

| 20 | My wife deserves an award for all the things she does to help me. | D |
| | I'm sometimes amazed at how thoughtful my wife's gifts to me are. | C |

| 21 | I love having my wife's undivided attention. | B |
| | Keeping the house clean is an important act of service. | D |

| 22 | I look forward to seeing what my wife gives me for my birthday. | C |
| | I never get tired of hearing my wife tell me that I am important to her. | A |

| 23 | My wife lets me know she loves me by giving me gifts. | C |
| | My wife shows her love by helping me catch up on projects around the house. | D |

| 24 | My wife doesn't interrupt me when I am talking, and I like that. | B |
| | I never get tired of receiving gifts from my wife. | C |

| 25 | My wife can tell when I'm tired, and she's good about asking how she can help. | D |
| | It doesn't matter where we go, I just like going places with my wife. | B |

| 26 | I love having sex with my wife. | E |
| | I love surprise gifts from my wife. | C |

| 27 | My wife's encouraging words give me confidence. | A |
| | I love to watch movies with my wife. | B |

| 28 | I couldn't ask for any better gifts than the ones my wife gives me. | C |
| | I just can't keep my hands off my wife. | E |

| 29 | It means a lot to me when my wife helps me despite having other things to do. | D |
| | It makes me feel really good when my wife tells me she appreciates me. | A |

| 30 | I love hugging and kissing my wife after we've been apart for a while. | E |
| | I love hearing my wife tell me that she believes in me. | A |

A: _____ B: _____ C: _____ D: _____ E: _____

A = Words of Affirmation   B = Quality Time   C = Receiving Gifts
D = Acts of Service   E = Physical Touch

INTERPRETING AND USING
YOUR PROFILE SCORE

Your primary love language is the one that received the highest score. You are "bilingual" and have two primary love languages if point totals are equal for any two love languages. If your second highest scoring love language is close in score but not equal to your primary love language, then this simply means that both expressions of love are important to you. The highest possible score for any one love language is 12.

You may have scored certain ones of the love languages more highly than others, but do not dismiss those other languages as insignificant. Your wife may express love in those ways, and it will be helpful to you to understand this about her.

In the same way, it will benefit your wife to know your love language and express her affection for you in ways that you interpret as love. Every time you or your wife speak each other's language, you score emotional points with one another. Of course, this isn't a game with a scorecard! The payoff of speaking each other's love language is a greater sense of connection. This translates into better communication, increased understanding, and, ultimately, improved romance.

If your wife has not already done so, encourage her to take The Five Love Languages Profile for Wives, which is available on page 183. Discuss your respective love languages, and use this insight to improve your marriage!

PROFILE FOR WIVES

Words of Affirmation, Quality Time, Receiving Gifts, Acts of Service, or Physical Touch? Which of these is your primary love language? The following profile will help you know for sure. Then you and your husband can discuss your respective love languages and use this information to improve your marriage!

The profile consists of 30 pairs of statements. You can only pick one statement in each pair as the one that best represents your desire. Read each pair of statements, and then, in the right-hand column, circle the letter that matches up with the statement you choose. It may be tough at times to decide between two statements, but you should only choose one per pair to ensure the most accurate profile results. Once you've finished making your selections, go back and count the number of times you circled each individual letter. List the results in the appropriate spaces at the end of the profile. Your primary love language is the one that receives the most points.

1	Sweet notes from my husband make me feel good.	A
	I love my husband's hugs.	E
2	I like to be alone with my husband.	B
	I feel loved when my husband washes my car.	D
3	Receiving special gifts from my husband makes me happy.	C
	I enjoy long trips with my husband.	B
4	I feel loved when my husband helps with the laundry.	D
	I like it when my husband touches me.	E
5	I feel loved when my husband puts his arm around me.	E
	I know my husband loves me because he surprises me with gifts.	C
6	I like going most anywhere with my husband.	B
	I like to hold my husband's hand.	E
7	I value the gifts my husband gives to me.	C
	I love to hear my husband say he loves me.	A
8	I like for my husband to sit close to me.	E
	My husband tells me I look good, and I like that.	A
9	Spending time with my husband makes me happy.	B
	Even the smallest gift from my husband is important to me.	C
10	I feel loved when my husband tells me he is proud of me.	A
	When my husband helps clean up after a meal, I know that he loves me.	D
11	No matter what we do, I love doing things with my husband.	B
	Supportive comments from my husband make me feel good.	A

12	Little things my husband does for me mean more to me than things he says.	D
	I love to hug my husband.	E
13	My husband's praise means a lot to me.	A
	It means a lot to me that my husband gives me gifts I really like.	C
14	Just being around my husband makes me feel good.	B
	I love it when my husband gives me a massage.	E
15	My husband's reactions to my accomplishments are so encouraging.	A
	It means a lot to me when my husband helps with something I know he hates.	D
16	I never get tired of my husband's kisses.	E
	I love that my husband shows real interest in things I like to do.	B
17	I can count on my husband to help me with projects.	D
	I still get excited when opening a gift from my husband.	C
18	I love for my husband to compliment my appearance.	A
	I love that my husband listens to me and respects my ideas.	B
19	I can't help but touch my husband when he's close by.	E
	My husband sometimes runs errands for me, and I appreciate that.	D
20	My husband deserves an award for all the things he does to help me.	D
	I'm sometimes amazed at how thoughtful my husband's gifts to me are.	C
21	I love having my husband's undivided attention.	B
	I love that my husband helps clean the house.	D
22	I look forward to seeing what my husband gives me for my birthday.	C
	I never get tired of hearing my husband tell me that I am important to him.	A

23	My husband lets me know he loves me by giving me gifts.	C
	My husband shows his love by helping me without me having to ask.	D

24	My husband doesn't interrupt me when I am talking, and I like that.	B
	I never get tired of receiving gifts from my husband.	C

25	My husband is good about asking how he can help when I'm tired.	D
	It doesn't matter where we go, I just like going places with my husband.	B

26	I love cuddling with my husband.	E
	I love surprise gifts from my husband.	C

27	My husband's encouraging words give me confidence.	A
	I love to watch movies with my husband.	B

28	I couldn't ask for any better gifts than the ones my husband gives me.	C
	I love it that my husband can't keep his hands off me.	E

29	It means a lot to me when my husband helps me despite being busy.	D
	It makes me feel really good when my husband tells me he appreciates me.	A

30	I love hugging and kissing my husband after we've been apart for a while.	E
	I love hearing my husband tell me that he missed me.	A

A: _____ B: _____ C: _____ D: _____ E: _____

A = Words of Affirmation   B = Quality Time   C = Receiving Gifts
D = Acts of Service   E = Physical Touch

INTERPRETING AND USING
YOUR PROFILE SCORE

Your primary love language is the one that received the highest score. You are "bilingual" and have two primary love languages if point totals are equal for any two love languages. If your second highest scoring love language is close in score but not equal to your primary love language, then this simply means that both expressions of love are important to you. The highest possible score for any one love language is 12.

You may have scored certain ones of the love languages more highly than others, but do not dismiss those other languages as insignificant. Your husband may express love in those ways, and it will be helpful to you to understand this about him. In the same way, it will benefit your husband to know your love language and express his affection for you in ways that you interpret as love. Every time you or your husband speak each other's language, you score emotional points with one another. Of course, this isn't a game with a scorecard! The payoff of speaking each other's love language is a greater sense of connection. This translates into better communication, increased understanding, and, ultimately, improved romance.

For information on the two-session (approximately 30 minutes each) video version of *The Five Love Languages*, contact:

LifeWay Press
127 Ninth Avenue, North
Nashville, TN 37234
Phone: 800/458-2772
www.lifeway.com

Each video package includes two copies of the *Viewer Guide* and a copy of the book.

In addition to Dr. Chapman's writing, he regularly conducts a weekend marriage enrichment seminar entitled *Toward a Growing Marriage*. The format is Saturday 9:00 a.m. - 3:30 p.m. For current seminar schedule, please visit:

www.moodyconferences.com

or write to:

Moody Conference Ministries
820 N. LaSalle Blvd.
Chicago, IL 60610
Phone: 312/329-4407

For information and schedule in other locations, write:

Chapman Seminar, MSB199
127 Ninth Ave., North
Nashville, TN 37234
Phone: 615/251-2277

We hope you enjoyed this product from
Northfield Publishing. Our goal at Northfield
is to provide high quality, thought provoking
and practical books and products that connect
truth to the real needs and challenges of
people like you living in our rapidly changing
world. For more information on other books
and products written and produced from a
biblical perspective write to:

Northfield Publishing
215 West Locust Street
Chicago, IL 60610